Life Plan? Trash Can

STEPHANIE DUCHAINE
MONTGOMERY

Dedicated to all of the young women who feel the pressure to settle down and figure things out

Life Plan? Trash Can

How I Learned to Embrace the Unpredictable
(and How You Can, Too!)

STEPHANIE DUCHAINE
MONTGOMERY

TABLE OF CONTENTS

INTRODUCTION

My guess is, we may have some things in common. At one point or another, you've probably made the wrong decision or dated (and/or settled for) the wrong person. Maybe you didn't get a job you knew would be perfect for you, only to feel like your dreams were slipping further and further away - or maybe society is telling you that the kind of person that you are doesn't exist and that you should conform to an industry or societal norm.

Over the last 15 years, I managed to navigate from a 2.7 GPA in high school to a top 25 university. I then managed to get a job at Google, only to quit and weasel my way into the entertainment industry. I met "my person" a decade later than expected. And it all happened thanks to twists and turns that I couldn't predict, and all while forgetting to appreciate my own individual journey.

I'd wanted to be an actress, or on camera in some capacity, for as long as I can remember. Even at a very young age, when I was on stage or in front of a camera, it was like I was in another world. The day would go by in a snap and I'd be in a state of euphoria afterwards, with an indescribable feeling that reaffirmed everything I knew to be true about my calling in life. It's kind of like that scene in

Happy Gilmore when Chubbs tells Happy to go to his "happy place." Once you get even the smallest taste of your own personal "happy place," it's impossible to forget it.

I started doing community theater when I was young (which I absolutely loved), and immediately mapped out my master plan - I'd graduate high school and go to college in New York or Los Angeles, where I'd study theater and become a famous actress. I'd get married at 25 and have four kids, ideally two girls and two boys just like my parents had. We'd have a medium-sized dog and a nice house in the suburbs, and life would be a perfect balance of career and family. Because that's what people do!

As it happens, not long after solidifying said master plan, the inevitable detours began. I didn't go to New York or Los Angeles after I graduated high school. I moved to Michigan and went to a community college, followed by the University of Michigan where I studied psychology and then got a job at Google. I finally moved to L.A. when I was 27, a grandmother in Hollywood years. I soon found myself at 30, unmarried with no children (much less four), in a healthy relationship with Starbucks, red wine and my MacBook.

Whether society is to blame or we singlehandedly create plans for what we want our life to look like, it's not uncommon to have a complete map that ends up needing to get thrown right in the garbage. Let me tell you, I fought this fact for years. Whether settling at the wrong job, staying in the wrong relationship or pretending like my internal warning signs weren't valid, it's been an ongoing battle to trust that whatever path my life takes is the right one.

Following my dreams hasn't been easy. Quite the contrary. It's been stressful and defeating. It's led to sleepless nights and many internal debates - should I just throw in the towel and go with something safe? In the end, though, perseverance through the doubts has never failed me.

In my fight to pursue my dreams of creating and performing, I've risked every good job I've ever had. I gave up a dream job at Google where I worked on innovative, exciting projects in order to be The LG Girl, the spokesperson for LG Mobile phones. I then gave up being The LG Girl in order to pursue a career in entertainment and television, eventually (after extensive rejection) hosting shows and segments for clients from People Magazine and the Home Shopping Network to Travelers Insurance and Amazon. I've also had some incredible comedic opportunities, including acting in a comedy series for Fox Sports and training at The Groundlings. All of these opportunities, however, were coupled with months of zero income and radio silence.

I broke into the industry of my dreams in some of the most unlikely ways. On paper, my path doesn't make sense. In reality, it was the only way that I could have gotten to where I needed to be.

Life Plan? Trash Can acts as gentle, comedic reassurance that while nothing ever looks the way that you thought it would, everything that you go through leads you to exactly where you need to be. And, that with a little determination, faith and perseverance, you can accomplish anything - a successful career, a happy family or, shoot…the most historic World Series in the history of baseball.

Let's get this party started, shall we?

ONE

(Belated) Quarter-Life Crisis

I spent my 30th birthday at Disneyland, wearing a pretty pink plastic crown.

While I'm not normally the kind of person that would choose to celebrate in such a way, this glorious decision was made for two reasons.

First, I was in a wild headspace and I'm convinced that my family was concerned about my mental stability. I was seemingly having my "quarter-life crisis" a bit later than expected, as I was transitioning into the "completely self-employed, uncertainty around every corner" stage of my career (I like stability). I was single (which was seemingly frowned upon at that age), and I was in a city and industry that was completely overwhelming (Hollywood, you are a horrible but beautiful bitch). What can I say? I had started to panic.

Second, according to those close to me, turning 30 was a big deal and needed to be celebrated accordingly. Admittedly, I still don't totally understand why 30 was such a milestone. I could already watch R-rated movies, drink, and rent a car. Was celebrating 30 just about the sheer fact that I'd survived the chaos of my 20s? If so, good job me. In retrospect, I suppose that was quite the feat.

It's not lost on me that I've had many opportunities in life and that I've been infinitely lucky, #blessed, or whatever you want to call it. My struggles were many times due to my attitude as opposed to solely my situation, and therefore I felt like there was no excuse to not pull my head out of my ass and start fresh with a Disneyland kickoff. So, down flew my family from Seattle to join me, my sister and her then-fiancé in Los Angeles and away we went to the happiest place on earth.

Regardless of how you feel on your birthday, let me tell you: Disneyland is *the* place to be. As soon as you show up, it's essential to start by telling the person taking your ticket that it's your birthday.

You'll then get a birthday button that they write your name on and everyone that you're with gets a button that says "I'm Celebrating." Add in the previously mentioned pink princess crown, mine being a gift from my mother, and you're immediately set up for success.

I've never been told "Happy Birthday" more times in my life. How depressed can you be when you're 30 years old and people are calling you a "birthday princess" for 12 hours, sometimes yelling it clear across the park? You can't. Try it. "Happy birthday, Birthday Princess!" Thank you. Thank you very much. By the end of the day I could see a twinge on each member of my family's face when someone said "birthday princess" for the 500th time, but because of my previous high stress levels they just smiled and asked the birthday princess which ride she wanted to go on next.

My family gets very strategic when planning a trip to Disneyland. We all feel that it's very important to maximize happy time by efficiently planning which rides to haul ass to when you first get to the park, as well as which Fastpass to get and when. Due to its rave reviews, we decided to start in Cars Land - and we then spent the rest of the day running around the park and, of course, frequenting the Indiana Jones ride.

This was a no-brainer for me, because in my opinion it's the best ride at Disneyland made even better by the fact that I have a massive crush on Indiana Jones. Being 30, single and spending some quality time swooning over a fictional character was something that I didn't find to be abnormal which, as I write this, is a little concerning.

The day was eventful, to say the least. First of all, my brother-in-law was recovering from the flu, and though he'd been violently throwing up for the past 24 hours, he insisted on coming along with us to celebrate my birthday with me and my family. Everything was ok until mid-afternoon, when I suggested that we go on Star Tours as my memory was telling me that it was a fun, smooth ride with a cute storyline that would let us all just relax and enjoy.

If you've ever been on Star Tours, you know that it's a violent, jerky ride as the Starspeeder goes on a wild rampage through space thanks to a few mistakes from the Star Wars crew. How he didn't puke, I'll never know.

My mother, who doesn't like roller coasters or anything like them, was also less than thrilled. It's no secret that my mom isn't much of a daredevil at amusement parks and, to be fair, she'd already had her fair share of adventures at this magical place. This of course includes the time that I peed my pants on the Submarine Voyage ride when I was two and when I screamed "Peter Pan, don't like 'em!" while crying hysterically on Peter Pan's Flight.

When my 30th birthday hit, I'd been avoiding alcohol for the previous month, in part because every time I did try to have a drink during that time everything was heightened, and I soon after found myself crying or in some other form of wild emotion. On my birthday, I decided that I wanted a beer with lunch and that I was going to have one because I was a strong, independent woman and it was my 30th birthday and damn it, I do what I want.

When it arrived, I began to make a toast to thank my family for coming down to Disneyland and being there for me. Before I even took a drink, I started to tear up because I was truly grateful that everyone was there celebrating with me.

It was really special to have them all there, but because they'd all seen me cry more than once in recent times, they immediately threatened to take the beer away. This was also shortly after my decision to try Botox, and crying with a frozen forehead is not pleasant as your muscles refuse to show the proper emotion, though tears are flowing down your face. I stopped crying.

At one point or another, I'd felt all of the "turning 30" emotions. Mad about decisions I'd made in my 20s, frustrated about not yet being where I thought I'd be, happy that I was now past certain stages of my life. Somehow, amid the chaos, uncertainty and everything else that had led up to that moment, my 30th birthday at Disneyland surrounded by my family was one of the best days of my life. Something changed inside of me on that day, which is a testament to the importance of family, your surroundings and being able to envision the kind of life that you want, even if you're not there yet.

Later that night as I sat alone in my apartment, I reflected on the last 30 years of my life. I thought about the lessons that I'd learned the hard way and I realized that I'd spent so much time trying to push forward and analyze every little thing that I'd forgotten to live a little and focus on my own happiness. I wondered why it took me so long to get where I was at that exact moment, and why I'd been constantly trying to fix broken things instead of choosing the happy, smoother path. And I realized that if I had felt so much stress and struggle, I knew that others probably did, too.

The truth is, I've never done anything the easy or traditional way. My life, potentially like many of yours, has been less of going from A to B and more of going from A to C, by way of E, passing by J on my way back to B wondering why there is always so much chaos.

On that note, I've always had a really hard time describing myself or fitting myself into an appropriate box. I grew up acting and my goal was always to be in the entertainment industry, where I am now, but I also love nerdy things and I used to work at Google.

Stark differences like these make up the person that I am and, over time, I've started enjoying the fact that I don't fit into a box. In hopes of providing a few laughs and especially some reassurance that no one has it all figured out, welcome to my stories about the growing pains, chaos and lessons learned over the last three decades (and then some). I do want to mention that this is, ironically, being written while living in a city where everyone my age lies and says that they're in their 20s.

TWO

The Earliest of Influences

Early childhood is a very interesting thing. Our minds start to develop while we're still in the womb and, while we can't remember a huge chunk of what happened in our early years, our little brains are taking everything in one second at a time. This stage of life starts to mold us into the people that we will become, though we have very little awareness about what's happening.

Before I was born, my parents had moved to Monterey, California from mid-Michigan after my father was transferred at work. Knowing how long it's taken me to fully acclimate to each new city I've moved to, I am very impressed at the thought of them leaving their hometown and setting up shop across the country well before the age of FaceTime, emails and text messages.

They then had their first kid not long after - a little pipsqueak with blonde ringlets and ears that stuck straight out, which was cute in a "whoa, look at those!" kind of way. Me.

I wore frilly socks and black patent leather Mary Janes, every single day. I don't care what the occasion was or where we were going, those shoes were my absolute favorite and I was perfectly comfortable wearing them with any outfit, any time.

I am still proud of the fact that I was the first girl to be born on my dad's side of the family in 93 years. Everyone thought I was going to be a boy, but what can I say, I like to keep people guessing. Gotcha, suckas. A few years later my sister Natalie was born, and my brother Brian soon after. They're 15 months apart and I'm not sure how my mom is still a sane individual after having three kids under the age of 5 (plus our faithful dog Max) while my dad worked long hours.

Because I was so young when we lived there, most of my memories are the weird, vague kind of memories. Like throwing up in the middle of the night during a sleepover at my friend's house after watching *The Little Mermaid.* Or sitting behind the bleachers collecting rocks during one of my dad's little league games.

My dad coached little league baseball at the park across the street, and sports of some kind were always on in the house. Maybe it was the slow pace (hey MLB, some of us like that kind of thing) or the constant social gathering of it all, but baseball (as a fan) always calmed me and made me feel at home. Probably explains why I cried sappy tears while watching the movie *Moneyball.* "Jeremy's about to realize the ball went 60 feet over the fence." *cue the waterworks*

After watching *Rookie of the Year* when I was eight or nine, I proclaimed that I would be the first female in the MLB. Those dreams were obviously never realized, though I was able to play in a charity softball game once and not completely embarrass myself. Victory is sweet.

To be fair, I should note that I was also determined to become a doctor after watching a medical drama on TV. And then a hockey player after seeing *The Mighty Ducks*. It was after that movie that it finally clicked that I didn't want to *be* those things, I wanted to *act* like those things - thus confirming my desire to become an actress, *dahling.* ("Actress, dahling" must be said with an English accent for full effect. I don't know why, it just does. I don't make the rules.)

Regardless, from counting rocks behind the bleachers to listening to my dad tell the story of how the 1989 Loma Prieta earthquake (the big, Bay Area one) took place during the A's/Giants

World Series, baseball is a good example of how something unlikely can provide support and stability, sneaking into our brains and hearts before we are even old enough to realize it.

When I was growing up in Monterey, both of my parents turned the age that I am as I write this. They had fallen in love years before, married young and spent every penny they had to rent a tiny fixer-upper house so that they could start a family - and here I was in a completely different place than they were at the time.

For a while, that really got to me. Why am I different? What's taking me so long to figure things out? Why don't I have kids by now? And above all else, why did I care so much?

I found myself stressing about so many things that haven't happened, and may *never* happen. I've found that so many of us second guess our decisions, worry about the future or stress over why we haven't yet accomplished the items on our life checklist. My answer was always that I liked to be prepared, but what is the benefit of worrying?

In general, I've now adopted the belief that if you're doing your best and actively trying to make something of yourself, you're doing *great*. Everyone has a different path, and there is no right way to live life other than the best way that you know how - all while doing your best to have faith that as long as you're putting one foot in front of the other, things will happen.

I really do mean one foot in front of the other. Baby steps. As evidenced in the upcoming chapters, sometimes accomplishing different tasks and goals may take much longer than anticipated, but, as Confucius once said, "It does not matter how slowly you go as long as you do not stop." Helpful when it comes to this book, which is going on three years before it's published. Lord help me.

What I learned from my days of patent leather Mary Janes:

1) If you want to wear patent leather shoes all day every day, you should do it. There are so many rules nowadays and sometimes you gotta just say screw it, I'm wearing my frilly socks.

2) Baseball will now be a part of my life forever and I'm glad my dad exposed me to it when I was little. When I was a kid I was in it for the sunflower seeds. Now I'm also in it for a guy that I love (but still the sunflower seeds).

3) Just keep swimming.

4) Do you, man. Who cares what's practical or what the "norm" is. If there's something that makes you happy and that isn't hurting anyone, go for it. Other people's negative opinions about you aren't your problem.

THREE

The Childhood Absence of Fear

I was five when my family moved from Monterey up to Seattle, Washington and the next stages of life presented a whole new ballgame. According to the psychologist Erik Erikson (I studied psychology in college, it fascinates me), the stage of development from age five to age 12 is heavily focused on competence and figuring out how to navigate this giant world of people and things. It's a wild world in which you're suddenly old enough to make your own decisions and you have more freedom to do things without being watched like a hawk.

When we first moved, we lived in a little house just west of the city. One thing that immediately comes to mind about this house was that I had a trundle bed that was pink and white, and my sheets matched my wallpaper. Each of these were white with small pink tulips that looked like polka dots if you stood far enough away. There was a red Japanese tree in the front yard just to the left of the slightly sloped driveway and it had a little backyard that was the perfect size for me and my siblings.

My brother Brian wasn't even two and still in a crib, and my sister Natalie and I shared the trundle. I got the top/real bed because I was three and a half years older, though I never stopped wondering if that was the best choice. The bottom bed just magically pulled out of nowhere, which did have a certain cool factor attached to it.

We've never called my sister by her real name as Brian couldn't initially say "Natalie," so he called her Nanny. Nanny was shortened to Nan, and this is the name she still goes by in the family. One day, Nan and I were playing in the backyard, drawing unidentifiable pictures with sidewalk chalk when my dad came home with a foreign looking plastic box with some wires that attached to it. We weren't particularly interested, until we heard a foreign type of music and ran inside to see 8-bit characters dancing around on the TV. Game over. We couldn't look away.

It was the original NES console, and we sat and watched for hours as my dad played through the original *Super Mario Bros.* levels. Watching him beat castle eight before Googling cheats was an option was incredible and, to this day, he's still the *Super Mario Bros.* champion in my mind.

From then on, we'd fight over who would get to play, and before long it was obvious that my dad had created three little gamer monsters. I think it's safe to assume that he got busted for it by my mom, though I have no proof. As the games rolled out, we'd beg to be able to play the newest ones and, over time, we were each masters of our different games: I could absolutely destroy *Super Mario 3* and *Zelda,* and Brian was the king of sports games like *RBI Baseball* and *Ice Hockey.*

Continuing on with the psychological assessment of this time, Erikson also says that ages five to 12 are when we begin to develop significant interpersonal relationships with people outside of the family, such as close neighbors. In our case this was completely accurate, as we loved running around the neighborhood and playing with the neighbor kids and their toys. We had great neighbors who were very sweet and welcoming, some of them with great candy drawers. (I love a good candy drawer. None will ever be better than my Grandma Peggy's, though, which is more of a candy basket. It's the best.)

It was all fun and games until one day I decided that I wanted to try and be coordinated, so I asked if I could borrow one of our neighbor's scooters. It had fun little blue tassels on the handlebars, though the grip was uneven and some of the metal exposed due to some of the rubber being peeled back. I didn't care, I was just happy to have the chance to be wild and free and feel the wind in my hair, which was now a darker shade of brown and more wild waves than bouncy curls.

Another thing about being this age: a complete absence of fear. Being a kid, you don't focus on how you might mess up or what other people are thinking about you, you just go for it and hope to experience something awesome and, many times, you do. I wish that I'd been able to continue this attitude into my 20s (and beyond). Life would have been so much easier, and probably a lot more fun.

All right, so I jumped on the scooter. For a few short seconds I felt the rush of rolling freedom, which was promptly halted as I fell and the exposed metal on the handlebar jammed into the forehead. There was blood everywhere. I don't recall the process of my neighbors calling my mother, but on the way to the doctor's office to get stitches I do remember asking my mom if I could swear. My outward reasoning was that I was not happy and that I thought it would help, though really I just wanted to see what I could get away with at the time. I tend to attempt to push limits here and there. What can I say?

After some hesitation, she gave me permission to say "the D word or the S word" and, upon realizing that I had options, I told her I preferred to save that for a later time. And did I ever. For a good stretch of my life I had a terrible mouth that has since gone in waves of cleanliness. My ability to figure out how to get what I wanted apparently developed early.

I've always liked to push the limits. I don't actively try to break the rules or cause problems, but I do think there's some benefit to questioning why things are the way they are and seeing if there is any leeway. I've found that a good chunk of the time I end up being able to accomplish things much more efficiently that way. And besides, you never really know what you can accomplish unless you ask. Case in point: I knew swearing was wrong, but the worst thing that could happen was she'd say no.

If I had to pick one thing that I wish I would have been able to hold onto from this time period, it's the aforementioned lack of fear. Even after the scooter mishap, my instinct at the time wasn't to avoid scooters, it was to show off my cool stitches. What happens to that feeling when we get older? It starts to dwindle as we begin to worry about what could go wrong, what others will think of us and the potential of failure.

I swear, at one point in my life I could have been crowned the Fear Queen. I stressed out about the potential outcome of everything. Everything! What if I went one way and it failed? What if I put myself out there and everyone laughed at me? What if I left a great, stable job to follow my dreams and everything crashed and burned? What if I wrote a book, and everyone hated it? "Ugh, all valid questions," I'd thought. The last question even led me to sit on this book for almost two years after I'd finished the first draft before actually doing something with it.

I consider myself to be a confident person but, sometimes, the fear of looking like an idiot crippled me. And sometimes it's still something I have to work to get past. Whether it's trying out a new character in the theater or simply coming up with an Instagram post, the fear of failure or rejection is something that I'm constantly working to overcome.

Here's what I know for sure, though - even if you try and fail, you've learned. You've learned how to better approach the situation, or you've learned to try a different path. You've learned one way that doesn't work. And you learn how to try again.

My goodness, the amount of time in my life that I've spent pondering a social media post wondering if it was cool enough or funny enough is ridiculous. Wondering if anyone would "get" the caption or how it would make me look. Wondering if I should share my work online because - gasp! - what if no one liked it?

What I learned from the NES days is that the things around you are amazing, like scooters and cutting edge technology, and you should experience them without fear. I also learned that we can't make decisions based on the perceived thoughts of other people. We can't live in fear, nor can we perform in hopes that people will like us. We can't create in hopes others will be receptive and we can't change who we are. So, then, the only thing we can do is to be authentic to our true selves and be excited about life, and, over time, the fear of failure begins to fade.

FOUR

The Goldfish

I don't do most things the smooth, traditional way. I imagine that's true for many of us. I don't immediately understand or adopt new trends and my life path has been far from your "standard" go to college, get married, buy a house, have kids. It takes me longer to do everything, in part because I rely mainly on my gut instinct and, when I don't like what it has to say, I've had the tendency to ignore it and try other things. Which never works. The more you fight your gut, the more you're just prolonging the inevitable.

In part because of this and in part because life can never be scripted and planned for, my dreams and visions are executed very slowly and, for a while, that drove me absolutely insane. Everyone loves instant gratification and seeing results quickly, and I am no exception. Only problem is that my life is the complete opposite in just about every way. I lay my foundation with a million steel LEGOs instead of a few big building blocks, which occasionally makes me want to beat my head against the wall, though I've found that when you build in such a way the stability of the foundation is quite sturdy.

If you would have asked me freshman or sophomore year of high school what I wanted to do for college, I would have surely told you that I was going to go to a four-year school, probably in Los Angeles or New York so that I could also study acting and become a famous actress.

When I hit senior year and it was time to make some decisions, however, I realized that I was in no position whatsoever to do something like that. I had prioritized my social life over my academics, one of the many foolish decisions that I'd made that cause me to look back at that time in my life and cringe. Other choices on that list include having my first beer when I was 14 (and clocking in just under 100lbs) and getting stoned soon after.

Quite frankly, I thought being drunk was fun but being stoned was terrible. My brain never stops trying to process and analyze as it is, and adding paranoia to the mix was not pleasant for me. In general, I'm shocked that I didn't get into any life-changing trouble in high school. Proof that there is a God, as far as I'm concerned.

Important to note, though, was that while I was super focused on being one of the cool kids, being on the cheerleading squad and going to the fun parties, I also spent my free time playing video games and asking my dad to drive me to the Sprint PCS store in downtown Seattle, weekly, to look at any potential new phones they had in stock. Phones with black-and-white screens and no internet capabilities, mind you. This is where it all began: the transition from NES geek to super nerd.

Meanwhile in the right side of my brain, I'd wanted to be an actress since I was a small child. I was in my first play in kindergarten and I lived life according to my theatrical passions. "All the world's a stage!" was, I'm sure, my subconscious motto and, though I spent a significant amount of time at the Youth Theater Northwest, I wasn't quite able to "leave the drama for the stage" as my father likes to put it.

This drama would usually show itself after I'd do things like throw a party at my parents' house when they were out of town, or sneak out and take the family minivan in the middle of the night to drive through Wendy's before I had my license. Because in the scheme of life, *stealing* a car and illegally driving it to get a Junior Bacon Cheeseburger is well worth it, right?

My poor parents. I'm sorry, Mom and Dad. Do you still love me? Please circle one: yes / no / maybe.

By the time I graduated, I had many years of theater under my belt, but my academics were horrific and I couldn't even begin to wrap my head around what packing up and moving to Los Angeles would look like. After finally moving to L.A. when I was 27, the decision to wait is one that I am so glad I made because this place is a wild world of dysfunction and insanity (see: Chapter 12).

Instead, I slowly added to my college + adulthood puzzle by moving to small-town Michigan, where all of my extended family lives, and attending one of the hometown colleges in the area. It was a far cry from Hollywood in a "night and day difference" kind of way, but it was also the stepping stone that I needed to grow up. Was I thrilled to be moving there instead of Los Angeles? No, I wasn't - but had I never made this (kinda forced) decision I surely wouldn't have added the necessary LEGOs to the foundation.

After much internal struggle, Bay City did feel like the right decision as it was far enough away from my parents to gain some independence, but a place with close family in a city that I knew relatively well. I was 17 when I packed my bags and moved in with Lori, my mom's half-sister and one of my best friends growing up.

Bay City is my mom's hometown, and my dad grew up just across the bridge. Growing up, we'd spend all of our summers there, which is when Lori and I would spend the majority of our time together. She is two years older than me and always a few steps ahead of me in life, including the years when when she was wearing a 34C bra and I was wearing a 32AA and crying about it at night. It was a trying time.

When I hit my freshman year, we were both in college and she was a great student, a great athlete and in a stable relationship (they've now been married for over a decade). She had her life together, while I was immature with a dirty mouth, but she was very sweet and just kind of went with it. We lived in a small (but nice) two-bedroom, one-bathroom apartment on the top floor, above a 60-year-old man who lived with his mother who would comment on everything that we did, from having friends over to receiving packages ("What'ya got there?").

There are a few important things to note about my time in Bay City. First of all, I became a really good rollerblader.

That's a lie. I learned how to stand up and move forward on rollerblades and I didn't break any bones in the process. As we've established, I may not be the most coordinated person you've ever met, but my aunt Cathy gave me a pair of rollerblades and I still keep them in the trunk of my car for use once per decade. The streets are all very flat and well paved, both in the neighborhoods and at parks and such and since rollerblading was very much a "thing" in Bay City, I went with it.

Next, Lori and I loved watching *Friends* after spending hours wandering through Meijer going grocery shopping. Meijer is kind of like Target, but bigger and with more good stuff. So, by the time we were done, we were thoroughly exhausted and ready to binge watch our favorite show while eating Bagel Bites or individually wrapped steaks wrapped in bacon. I've never forgotten those weird steaks. They were under four dollars and were these tiny little cuts of filet with a single piece of bacon wrapped around them. I'd make one on the George Foreman Grill, wash it down with a Diet Vanilla Coke and feel very accomplished. Independence!

In our little apartment, we also had a fish tank with a few goldfish. One by one, they decided that they hated us and jumped out of the tank. Sometimes I'd come home to a dead fish on the floor that had seemingly committed suicide. More often than not, though, I'd come home to a random towel on the floor, which I quickly realized was actually a goldfish blanket, keeping our fish friend warm right where he or she had died because they'd jumped out and Lori had found them. Though it was technically her fish tank, she was never a fan of moving the fishies to their final resting places.

This was one of my first times having to take care of unpleasant adult things on my own. It was like when I was little (and by little I mean until the day I moved out) and a bug would crawl into my room and I'd run, start crying and ask my dad to save me from it. Except this was a fish, it was dead and if I cried no one was going to be there to help me out so I was forced to suck it up.

We spent every Sunday having dinner with my grandparents, Lori's parents. My grandma served the most comforting meals and we *always* had dessert. I think the cheesecake she'd serve was my favorite. She also always had the candy bowl I've already mentioned. My sweet tooth is out of control and the big tub of Laffy Taffys from Sam's Club that they always had was such a phenomenal thing.

To be more specific, the pink and purple Laffy Taffys. I'm a total cherry picker, and to this day will pick out the good colors of any candy and leave the rest. Some people get upset about this, but it makes no sense to me why anyone would eat the ones they don't really like, as this is not a "take the good with the bad" situation.

I am really thankful that my grandparents and extended family were close to me. While I constantly pretended like I was adult and mature enough to handle life on my own, that was absolutely not true. For a long time I had this attitude like I knew everything, and that I should know everything. Looking back, I don't know why I was so against taking advice or asking for help when I needed it. But life had a way of forcing me to, like when I came out of class one day and my car was dead.

I know absolutely nothing about cars. Zero. And of course as soon as I realized that I should call my grandfather, who worked for many years at General Motors and drove over immediately to help me out, my car started up like there was never a problem. Something about an electrical something? Seriously. I know nothing about cars.

One night a few months into living there, Lori and I drank some disgusting, cheap vodka, went to the 18-and-over club in Saginaw and then got into a water fight in a gas station bathroom before coming home and eating way too many Totino's Pizza Rolls. The next morning I woke up with a Popov hangover (ick) and realized that I was now an adult and, whatever I did in the future, no one was going to hold my hand.

It struck me that if I wanted to continue to have fun the way we'd had fun the night before, I needed to accept responsibility and make something of myself. I wanted to be able to do whatever I wanted, and to be able to afford to do whatever I wanted. Nights out ain't cheap, nor is travel, shoe shopping or a nice bottle of wine. So what's a girl to do? In my case, it was try out this whole school thing.

The class that I remember first succeeding in at Delta College was pre-Calculus, and I still don't know how that happened because math is not even close to being one of my strong points. I still have to whip out my phone to calculate the tip when I go to dinner. If I remember correctly, it was the first class that my young professor had ever taught, so I think he was feeling it out and being generous. Either way, I felt the rush of academic success after getting an 'A' that first semester and felt great having achieved something like that all on my own.

I'll never forget that classroom, or where I was sitting the first time I scored well on an assignment or when I realized that something that seemingly "wasn't my thing" was attainable if I worked for it.

And oh man, I had to put in the work. I spent hours analyzing that stupid pre-Calc book knowing full well I would most likely never again use it in my life. But the feeling that success was possible if I just put in the work outweighed any of that, and I started to feel almost addicted to the process. Study hard, get good grades, set myself up for future success.

Once I learned what it took to move forward academically and what the future implications of my studies could be, the unexpected puzzle pieces started falling into place. Spending more time at school, I started to make new friends. Getting better grades, I started to be able to take better classes. And as time went on, I started to see the potential opportunities for my future beginning to unfold, one day at a time.

I also felt pretty cool being the only kid with a flip phone that played the SportsCenter theme as a ringtone, which I'd paid for myself thanks to my part-time job working retail in the mall. After numerous threats, my parents had followed through with their promise of cutting me out of the family cell phone plan after I constantly overshot the allocated amount of text messages. This was just another clear sign of the true development of my addiction to (passion for?) technology.

After two years, I applied to the University of Michigan with a GPA of 3.97 – a far cry from where I'd started not that long before. I didn't totally believe it when I got the acceptance envelope, but once it sunk in, I felt incredibly accomplished. To this day, getting into U of M was one of my greatest accomplishments.

What I learned is that it doesn't matter where you start. It only matters that you DO start, that you work toward your goal and that you trust your process even when the future is unclear and you don't understand it. It took me four years of high school rebellion and two years of community college, but I'd gotten to that next level. And the journey continued.

FIVE

Fifi

Fifi (full name Fiona Marie Duchaine) was a 13-week-old, runt of the litter kitten when I heard that she needed a home. I was 19 with minimal income and in no real position to adopt an animal, but pssh, those were just small details.

She was living on a farm in the middle of nowhere and the family was desperate for her to find a home. After a shift at PACSUN, the surfer-central clothing store in the Bay City Mall, I drove out to said farm in the middle of nowhere in my 1995 forest green Oldsmobile to see this kitten. There were animals everywhere, and the unnamed cat was of course the one that refused to come out and sit with any of them.

The farmer's daughter disappeared for a minute and came back with a scrawny, sassy, black-and-white cat that looked afraid and like she'd claw your eyes out if you tried to pull something she didn't like. I named her Fifi and took her home with me.

I remember the family on the farm being relieved and, as I got into the car, I said "I promise that I'm going to take really good care of her." Though they knew nothing about me, the mother said "I know you will." I'm sure she was just happy to have found a home with someone who seemed even slightly responsible. That gave me a boost of confidence, and I figured this whole "cat mom" thing would be a piece of cake.

Instead, Fifi and I had our growing pains. She loved to Spider-Man her way up the curtains, leaving rips in her wake before walking across the curtain rod, which was well above my reach. She also loved to stick her head into any cup that was sitting around and went especially buckwild lapping up black coffee out of my mug. I'd never owned or spent time around cats before, but I assumed that it wasn't normal for a cat to enjoy a drink that even most humans I know much won't consume without adding cream and sugar.

She would also only drink fresh water, usually out of a human's glass that they'd left unattended, or out of a running faucet. I was forced to leave a water glass on the floor by the door that I refilled each day, because a water bowl just wasn't sufficient for Miss Feline USA.

She was born with a strong personality. She liked what she liked and hated everything else, with no apologies. As cats are, she may have also been a little bipolar, evidenced by the fact that she was an incredible snuggler who would make you feel like the most important person in the world while purring into your collarbone, and then scratch the shit out of you when she'd had enough.

She was with me from Bay City to Ann Arbor, and then roadtripped with me to California. She traveled with me up to Seattle to visit my family (yes, I'm *that* girl who would fly with her cat) and she was my ride or die through all stages of my young adult life.

Pets are who they are, and they need what they need. They want love, attention, and food (which pretty much also sums up everything that I want on any given day) and there are some that could not care less what you think, and they don't think twice about it. And what do we do? We love and accept them. Acceptance and unconditional love - so easy to show our furry friends even when they poop all over the carpet, but sometimes so difficult when it comes to our fellow humans.

Sure, we train our pets. We teach them not to pee on the floor and we teach them not to scratch the couch or rip apart the carpet. But we don't try to change their personalities. We laugh when they're sassy or when they bark out of control at something they think they heard, and the good always outweighs the bad.

People, on the other hand, don't always get that courtesy. How many times to do we see the beliefs of others, and feel the need to change them or try to explain why they're wrong? The Twitter battles alone nowadays are exhausting. We seem to think that we can properly debate in a 280-character format, yelling at the other side about whatever they've put out there. Even worse, friendships now have the potential to be destroyed over political or religious beliefs. We've seemingly become completely divided over topics ranging from abortion to gay marriage and we've lost the ability to even come together and discuss.

I am a white woman and I will never know what black families, gay people or women who have had an abortion go through on a daily basis unless they're willing to tell their stories, and I'm willing to *listen*. Shit, I will never know what the fellow white girl sitting next to me is going through unless she wants to tell me. So if someone is a little sassy or someone has an aggressive viewpoint, why are we (myself included) sometimes so quick to judge?

Have we become incapable of agreeing to disagree? I don't know. What I do know is that I was able to give a little creature the benefit of the doubt more than I'm able to give some humans sometimes.

Fifi taught me unconditional love and a different side of acceptance. I could never sit her down and tell her why she needed to stop scratching the walls or stop doing the things she was instinctually programmed to do, nor could she explain to me why she does it. I just loved her and laughed when she spilled her water glass all over my wood floors for the 50th time.

What I learned, from an eight-pound cat, is that all you can really do is try not to mess up other people's stuff, be true to who you are, and give others the same courtesy.

SIX

Big Girl Pants

After some soul searching in Bay City, I was finally ready to put on my big girl pants and assume some real responsibility. Responsibility that went beyond paying my own cell phone bill. It was time to transfer to the University of Michigan.

If you'd asked me even one year before if I would ever be studying at such a great school, I would have laughed and made some sort of self-deprecating comment trying to pretend like I didn't give a shit about studying when in reality I would have been secretly destroyed that I had so little to show for myself, yearning for bigger and better things. The good news is, it's never too late to make a change, evidenced by the next few years of my life.

First things first, I needed to find somewhere to live. I didn't know the city of Ann Arbor well at that point, nor did I know anyone in the area. My dad came to town and we looked at a few places, the one we settled on being a two-bedroom apartment in the Lake Village complex. They were very sweet in the front office and always had cookies and fresh popcorn, which I took to be a very good sign.

The apartment itself was big with two bedrooms and two bathrooms, a washer and dryer, a patio and a dishwasher. This was an adult apartment and I couldn't help but feel like I was a becoming a real human being. Now, I just needed to find a roommate.

After asking around, a friend knew a friend who had a friend looking for someone to live with. Yes...you read that right. Little did I know that this girl four times removed would become one of my biggest forms of entertainment and a friend that would impact my life in more ways than I can count.

Nina is that girl that, like it or not, says what she thinks with no filter. She's supportive and loyal and will tell you your good qualities, when you look pretty, if she thinks you're in the wrong or if she hates your dress. She was a breath of fresh air among everyone who sugarcoated things, because she's genuine in her friendship but she's not interested in wasting time.

After we furnished the apartment with vintage furniture from my parents, we figured out the other logistics. She got the master bedroom, and to balance it out I got the parking spot in the assigned carport. For the rest of my years with roommates, I always wanted the parking spot. I will always take that kind of convenience over extra square footage. Always.

For a while, she did her thing and I did mine. She, a transfer from UCLA, was consistently appalled at my diet of frozen food and ranch dressing while I couldn't comprehend why anyone would want a giant pile of "greens" for dinner. She had a closet filled with nice clothes while I had T-shirts from Target (still a wardrobe staple) and more shoes than I knew what to do with.

After she'd surveyed the situation, Nina remarked that I had "100 pairs of shoes and nothing to wear them with." That was a fact. And I was fine with it. I've always loved shoes and it's only been in the last few years that I've actually started rounding out my closet with things to wear them with, only because some clients require you to bring your own wardrobe to set.

I don't want to say that I was uptight when I first met Nina, but...I was uptight when I first met Nina. I was a bit sheltered and didn't get out much, going from the suburbs of Seattle to small-town Michigan. She, however, was one of the popular kids who had already lived the city life in Los Angeles. She was on the tennis team, hung out with the cool kids, and was the Social Sally of the two of us. I, meanwhile, could usually be found in the library or on our couch wearing sweatpants and a super stylish hoodie typing away on my laptop, watching *Sex and the City*. I'd be in bed long before she'd get back from a Friday night out and turn on *MTV Jams* for the after party with her friends. Not being someone who likes conflict, Fifi and I stayed in my room.

While my patience has dwindled a little bit since college, generally speaking I'm all for people living their lives and doing whatever it is that they do. You do you, and I'll do me, and we'll be all good. Just don't mess with my sleeping or eating habits because crabby Stephanie is not a fun Stephanie. You've been warned.

I spent a lot of time hiding in my room, studying away. In this new situation, as long as I was in my own personal bubble where I felt safe, I was all good. By this time, I was also fully obsessed with mobile phones and computers and I'd bought my first Apple product (the iBook). I was perfectly content sitting in my room on the Internet trying to figure out what the heck this "The Facebook" thing was after Michigan became one of the first schools to join it. I remember being grossly uncomfortable when one of our neighbors came by and sat on my bed to small talk while I was on my computer, wondering what to do with someone being in my comfort zone without really being invited.

Soon enough, though, Nina began pulling me out of my shell. She made fast friends with our neighbors next door, Daniel and Chris, and Aaron, Kurt and his girlfriend (now wife) Kathleen who lived upstairs. She formed the relationships by randomly walking over, knocking on their door and striking up a conversation. I remember being shocked when she'd knock on a random person's door and strike up a conversation like she'd known them forever.

She would invite them over, and soon their friends would be over, too. Our apartment became the place to get together and have a drink or watch a game, and she'd convince me to come hang out, just for a bit. Before I knew it, I actually had friends of my own at Michigan. Let me tell you, game days are a lot more fun when you're not going by yourself or with that one kid you don't really know from your clinical psychology class.

The transition from loner to low-level socialite was uncomfortable but, by senior year, I was significantly less lame. I still loved my library time and spent plenty of hours there, but I also actually went out on Friday nights and started - *gasp!* - having fun.

My years at Michigan had a gigantic impact on who I am today. So much has happened since I graduated but, let me tell you, days at Michigan were *the* days. I miss them. I miss the Big House, I miss the people, and I miss the feeling of being young and having the most freedom you'll ever have to really live life with minimal worries while figuring out who you are and what you believe in.

It wasn't until the spring of my senior year that, after a six-year hiatus, I tried out for the first theater show since high school. I can't remember in the slightest what motivated me to do so, but someone told me they were holding auditions and I decided to go. I knew no one at the Ann Arbor Civic Theater, but that little internal whisper was loud enough to get my attention.

I was cast in the show *The Best Little Whorehouse in Texas,* and it was so much fun. The cast and crew were amazing and I made friends that I'm still in touch with to this day.

What I learned is a big one. I learned that if something is lying dormant inside of you, it only takes one match to relight the fire - even if it's not yet time for the fire to completely burn. We always feel like we need a massive blueprint mapped out if we want to make a life change, but we don't. We simply need to be willing to take baby steps in the right direction.

SEVEN

Smoke and Fire

I went on my first European "vacation" when I was a junior at Michigan. I put vacation in quotes because it was mainly two friends grossly out of their comfort zones trying their best to figure out where to go, what to do and what was happening. Spoiler alert: Being taken out of your comfort zone is when the most significant personal growth happens, and being a small-town girl in another country where she doesn't speak the language is a good start.

Emily is my friend from high school, and for her college graduation (she was a year ahead of me), she'd planned a six-week trip through Europe. My spring break lined up perfectly with the first leg of her trip, so I decided to tag along.

I'd be flying in from Detroit, and she from Seattle. Our 10-day plan was to meet in Amsterdam, spend some time there, and then take the train to Paris. We'd later take the train back up to Amsterdam where I'd fly home and she'd continue on to Prague, the next stop on her journey. We felt pretty good about our pre-trip planning, and, since I'd been studying French for the last few years, we figured we were probably going to be just fine.

We knew we were in for it when we landed in Amsterdam and couldn't read anything or speak to anyone. I had been thinking that Amsterdam was probably similar to England, and that everyone spoke English. Strike one. We spent the first couple of days just trying to make sure we didn't panic and die.

Our hotel room was small and simple. One tiny room, two twin beds, and a TV. We found a connection to home on one channel that wasn't in English but that seemed to be the Dutch version of MTV. One show was similar to "TRL" and we got our fix of *NSYNC and Backstreet Boys videos, which we were just happy were in English and something that we knew. We spent more time in the hotel than we should have, as the discomfort of being in a country where we didn't speak the language felt debilitating.

Going to the Red Light District and to a "special" cafe probably weren't the safest ideas at this point in our lives, but what can I say – my rebellious side wasn't dead yet and I pretended that I liked to live on the edge even though inside I was grossly uncomfortable. My mistake, because I will forever have the image burned into my brain of an old man masturbating on the street while a woman dancing in the window gestured for him to come inside.

Weed is legal in Amsterdam, so we'd figured we should probably go check out what these cafes were all about. We learned that they serve weed there much like a drink or a cup of coffee, just order it off of the menu and you're good to go.

We went up to the bar area and pretended like we knew what we were talking about. If anyone who actually smokes weed saw the joint that I tried to roll, they'd probably either laugh hysterically or else be really pissed because I had absolutely no clue what I was doing. Emily wasn't really interested in smoking weed but she was there for the experience, and thank God she was with me and sober because it got weird, fast.

I took maybe two hits, neither of which could have even been real considering the poor joint construction. Pretty soon I felt very strange and told Emily that we needed to leave because I was convinced that 1) they kept dimming the lights in the cafe and 2) that there was a big white dog running around behind the bar. Emily was terrified and I remember her looking at me and asking "Are you okay?" as we rode in a taxi back to our hotel, which really freaked me out. Thankfully, she put me to bed and I apologized to her in the morning. Strike two.

The next day, we walked over to a nearby grocery store. I don't know what it is about grocery stores, but I love wandering through them in any country because they always have different, great stuff. Take Canada, for example. A Canadian grocery store was the first time I found Yan Yans, Pocky and Frutios gummies, and Canada is now the only place that I can still find Dunkaroos, some of my absolute favorite treats (the vanilla chip, not the chocolate). Regardless of the location, grocery stores calm me.

As we walked into this Dutch grocery store, there was a man outside holding a stack of newspapers. He started aggressively handing one of them to me and I felt as though I had no choice but to accept it, until he then started aggressively yelling that I owed him money for it. I took one look at the paper and then awkwardly looked back at him and said "Well, I can't read this, so…" and shoved it back into his arms, startled. Emily and I laughed about that for days and it felt great to be in a position where we could loosen up and start to enjoy our surroundings a bit more.

Another memorable event on the trip took place on the train from Amsterdam to Paris, via Brussels. At one point, Emily and I had gotten comfortable in the seats at the front of the train car that I'd acquired for us by speaking broken French to a kind gentleman, asking him if he'd mind switching his assigned seat with Emily so that she and I could sit together. We both fell asleep.

We couldn't have been asleep for long when we heard shouting coming from the back of the train. Dazed, I tried to sleep through it but the yelling only got louder, until we both woke up and turned around to a completely empty train car, with the train itself at a dead stop. The conductor was running at us full speed screaming at us in who knows what language. "What?" I screamed. "I don't understand!"

He looked at us with panic in his eyes and screamed back "SMOKE, AND SMOKE, AND SMOKE – AND FIRE!" And when he put it that way, it was much easier to understand that THE TRAIN WAS ON FIRE.

We grabbed our things and ran off of the train onto an unknown platform. Let me tell you, two freaked out American girls stand out like a sore thumb among well-traveled Europeans, who were uninterested that the train was on fire and more just irritated that their schedules had been disrupted. To them, a train fire was merely a nuisance, but, to us, it caused a real panic that only began to subside when we found the one person that either spoke English or that just actually admitted to speaking English who was able to help us with new train tickets.

Stepping off the train into the city of Paris was a relief like none other, and I knew exactly what we needed to do. Eat delicious food, drink red wine and only take cabs for the foreseeable future regardless of the fact that my savings account was dwindling at an alarming rate.

As many people do, I fell in love with France and vowed to get back as often as possible. I ate baguettes and drank Coca Light (Diet Coke) every day, and we finished off our nights with French wine and *le canard* (duck) at the restaurant next to our hotel. It was fantastic and just like I'd always dreamed that it would be.

One of the hardest parts for both of us was feeling like we'd been completely cut off from the United States. Communication wasn't easy, as our cell phones had no roaming plans and the hotel outbound calling rates were insanely high. We tried to go to an Internet cafe to keep in touch via email, but, by the time we figured out how to use the European keyboards, our allocated time was up and we had to put in more money. With the time change, we also found ourselves not being able to get in touch with our family members, and many tears of discomfort were shed.

On our last day in Paris, Emily and I went to a *petit boulangerie* next to the train station and I got the most phenomenal strawberry tart that I'd ever seen or tasted. It was a real work of art and I have yet to find another tart that can even begin to compare. I savored every bite and as I sat there with Emily, I felt a sense of accomplishment and happiness.

As we left, feeling like we may have finally found our groove here in Europe, Emily tripped over a crack in the sidewalk and face-planted – hard – onto the Parisian sidewalk. I was slightly ahead of her so I didn't know what had happened until I heard a small child laughing hysterically and watched his mother grab his hand and step over my poor friend, lying there mortified. Strike three?

After hurrying to her side and helping her dust herself off, we walked back to the hotel in complete shock that we had made it to the end of our trip alive.

It's a very strange feeling being put into a situation where you're immediately forced out of your comfort zone and have no lifeline, but it's important and something that I think we should all strive to do more often because I've found that that's when the most personal growth truly happens. That statement is coming from a person who likes smoothness and stability, so I totally get that it's easier said than done and I still have to battle sometimes to take my own advice.

Two things have the potential of happening when I'm taken out of my comfort zone. The first is panic. Sheer, utter panic. The second is withdrawal. It's hilarious how many people first meet me and then later admit they assumed I was insanely shy because I didn't talk much. Just surveying the situation, people - the show is about to begin! Either way, when it's fight or flight, I'm a fighter. I think most of us are, or can be. We just have to be okay with the extreme discomfort that may come before that.

In the end, I flew back to the United States with a new sense of independence, financial responsibility (I'd paid for the trip on my own, down to my last penny), and pride. It was weird, ugly and my savings account was gone, but I survived being outside of my comfort zone in a real way and saw how incredible the world can be. Emily also became a friend for life and, when I make it back to Seattle to visit, she's one of the few people that I always make an effort to see.

What I learned from this trip is summed up with the quote, "If it doesn't challenge us, it doesn't change us." Yes, I sometimes get wildly uncomfortable when I step out of my comfort zone, to the point of moderate to severe anxiety - but I have found that during times that provoke such anxiety, I end up being a better, stronger or smarter person because of it.

EIGHT

Employment

As it goes for many students, my impending graduation from the University of Michigan set me into a bit of a panic. An unknown future was something that I didn't do well with at the time, and I knew that any sort of financial help from my parents would soon be gone. My part-time job, which paid for things like my cell phone, food and gas, wasn't going to cover all of my expenses.

I'd worked hard at Michigan, and I felt really good about the things I'd accomplished there. I graduated with a 3.67 (almost a full grade point from where I'd finished in high school!) and I'd been involved with some really great programs while I was there, like being a psychology peer advisor, which rounded out my resume. When I graduated, I applied to more companies that you would believe, and I felt pretty confident that my diploma and resume would speak for themselves!

They didn't. I didn't hear back from any company, anywhere.

I had been working part-time as a French teacher my junior and senior year at Language Adventure, a company that created and taught after-school language programs in elementary schools. When I graduated, the owner offered me a raise to $18,000 a year to work four days a week as her office manager. That would bring the official employee count up to two – the founder of the company, and me. I answered the phone, hired language teachers and handled other organizational duties. I was grateful for the opportunity.

Naturally, after months of not being able to pay someone to hire me, two weeks after accepting this job I got a call from Google.

Let's rewind a few months.

Just after I'd graduated, Google had advertised that they were opening a new office in Ann Arbor, and my excitement levels peaked. My dad got an NEC computer through his work in 1995, and nothing on this earth could stop me from staying up all hours of the night, logged onto AOL and having inappropriate conversations with classmates, playing Chip's Challenge and downloading illegal music.

Eventually I ruined that computer, most likely by downloading things on Napster, but I was that kid that bought old computers from the thrift store and did whatever I could to further feed my obsession (anyone remember Juno? Not the movie, the old CD for free internet access?). The thought of being able to get a job working at a company that I viewed as THE internet evoked feelings of pure, unadulterated joy.

I'd applied many months before, and one of the first steps was to fill out a quiz. It was a questionnaire of sorts, aiming to judge how I would handle different situations that I may find myself presented with. Apparently my answers were satisfactory, because a month or two later I was notified that I'd gotten an in-person interview.

I interviewed with many different people, all of whom were incredibly smart and charismatic. One part of the interview process that I remember most was being asked this question (shoutout to you, J. Nicoletti):

"If you were a contestant on *Jeopardy*, which five categories would you most like to answer?"

I can't remember all five, but I'm certain that three of them were brands of shoes, plus fitness equipment and sports trivia.

A few months had gone by and I hadn't heard anything, so I assumed that I hadn't gotten the job. I struggled to find a job and the panic *really* started setting in.

On top of the desire to start my post-collegiate life on a good, career-driven path, I also wanted to be financially independent as soon as possible. We've now established my stubborn and independent nature and, let me tell you - it's hard (impossible) to make 100 percent of your own decisions when you're reliant on someone else to fund your endeavors. If they're paying, they have a say. Usually a substantial say. Understandably, after supporting me financially through four years of college and living expenses, my parents had no interest in financing my shoe collection, froyo runs or my future "buy 6 bottles, save 10 percent" wine purchases at Safeway.

Naturally, after just having made a commitment to the sweet woman who had hired me as her office manager, I got an email from Google asking me when I could start.

I remember feeling this insane push and pull, knowing that I'd already made a commitment to the one person who had offered me a job when no one else did, but also knowing that I had this incredible opportunity in front of me. When I say I'm going to do something, I do it – so it was very hard for me to process how to quit the office manager job when I'd just assumed that responsibility.

As the wheels spun in my head, I had a conversation with a friend that really helped me put things into perspective. He helped me see that the most important thing here was going to be how I handled accepting a new position. I couldn't just drop everything and run, but if I gave her adequate notice and had an adult conversation about it, he was sure she'd be happy for me, albeit a little disappointed (Thank you, Ali. You were right).

It was a hard conversation to have, as it was my first experience having and quitting a real job, and feeling like I was letting someone down in that area. Exactly as Ali had predicted, though, she was disappointed but told me that it was absolutely an opportunity that I had to take. Google was willing to push my requested start date back a few weeks to accommodate my existing job, and I was able to solidify October 9, 2006 as my Google start date.

What I learned is that you never, ever, have to settle for something. As long as you respect those around you and handle any situations that arise in a respectful manner, you gotta do what you gotta do. It takes a lot of courage, but making the hard decisions can lead to incredible things.

NINE

Google

Soon enough, October 9th rolled around and I showed up to a tiny, startup-feeling office in downtown Ann Arbor. Being a satellite office, a small group of Googlers had come out from the Mountain View headquarters to get the office up and running. It was mainly advertising focused, and the first nine people to be hired (myself included) began policy training.

As I usually did in new situations, I kept to myself in the beginning, ate lunch at my desk and didn't socialize much. Though this specific way of approaching things has evolved and improved with age, I have, historically, had the tendency to hang back and subconsciously survey the situation before diving in and joining the party. My co-workers later laughed at the thought that they'd once taken me to be shy and reserved as I belted out "Tainted Love" (complete with choreography) in front of the entire company at the first ski trip that I attended.

As time went on, more and more people were hired and the original nine turned into a team of hundreds. Google opened a new, much larger office to accommodate all of the new teams and employees, and it was an unbelievable first experience working at a "real job."

A little over a year in, I was now in the full swing of the job. I had client relationships that I was managing and I helped launch the Ann Arbor chat support team. My co-workers were brilliant and funny, showcased not only through the work that they did but also through the Friday weekly social gatherings that would happen in the cafe at 4:30 p.m. Rock Band tournaments, karaoke, guest speakers, you name it - there was always something that made you smile. Not to mention the flowing food and drinks, too. Obviously another highlight.

At this point, I'd been living in Michigan for going on six years and, while I loved it, I was also starting to feel a pull back to the West Coast. My family was there, and both the distance and the fact that flying out of the Detroit airport was absurdly expensive helped ensure that I barely saw them. Furthermore, every now and then that pesky little whisper would speak up, reminding me that I was very far away from Hollywood.

The atmosphere at Google allowed for open communication between employees and their managers, and though it stressed me the heck out, I got the courage to talk to my manager about what had been going through my mind. I asked if there were any opportunities on the West Coast and what that might look like. They were beyond accommodating in helping me find my new home at their San Francisco office.

Through co-workers, I found a roommate who was also a Bay Area Googler. I was going to be paying exactly $1,000 more a month in rent for a room in an apartment in San Francisco compared to more space than you can imagine in a three-story condo in Ann Arbor. My "cost of living" raise wasn't that much, so for a while I was no stranger to a Subway "sub of the day" and a glass of cheap wine for dinner.

My new position was as an Account Manager on the Traditional Media team working on beta platforms that aimed to make traditional media advertising space (television ads, print ads and radio ads) available to purchase via an online interface. As with any beta product, there were bugs that needed ironing out, which sometimes ended up being my favorite thing.

Of course you never want the client to experience issues with the product or platform they're paying for, but I found myself in the zone when I'd be taking info from one of my clients and having to relay it and work with the engineers to come up with a solution. I respected their work immensely, and the feeling of helping to make things work in a technical sense, though I am far from an engineer, was very exciting for me.

Furthermore, a few months into working in the San Francisco office, one of my mom's childhood friends (from Bay City, Michigan) was in the Bay Area, working on the Mervyn's creative team. She landed me an audition for a Mervyn's commercial and, after a few rounds of auditions, I booked the job.

Now you tell me, on what planet does a friend of your mom, who grew up in a tiny town in Michigan that no one has ever heard of, end up being able to give you a break in one of the toughest industries to break into?

Most times, to get an audition like this, you need an agent. Your agent then submits your headshot and/or resume, at which point the client searches through all submissions from agencies around the city (and sometimes country) until they narrow down who they want to see in person. You then go through rounds of auditions before the client chooses a tiny percentage of people to act in the commercial.

Thanks to Julie, I still had to prove myself in the audition, but I was able to skip all of that agency stuff and get right to the nerve-racking, "be judged on the spot" round of auditions. It was overwhelming, exciting, and gave me completely unrealistic expectations for auditioning in the future (which I'll tell you about later).

I knew I was going to have to get Google's permission to take a day off to shoot, so I set up a meeting with my manager and awkwardly brought up the situation. Imagine my surprise when he said "What you do with your vacation days is your business." Hmm, so okay. You're telling me I can work at one of the best companies in the world, have all the perks in the world, and still sign with an agency and go out for commercial work. In whatever alternate universe I was living in, I wasn't about to argue.

On top of having a job that I really, really liked, Google is what everyone says it is in all other areas. You need a doctor? Walk downstairs. How about a massage? Sure, it's around the corner. Don't even get me started on the food. I'm sure I gained 10 pounds while I was there, despite the gym membership that was also paid for.

As time went on, though, I started to get antsy and feel out of place. The thought alone that something didn't feel right gave me extreme anxiety - I felt like there had to be something wrong with me. How could anyone possibly be unhappy with what I had?

The longer I tried to fight it, the stronger my feelings got. I remember walking down the hall one day after a meeting and feeling so pissed off. For no reason. A new manager on the team had said something that I didn't agree with and I just shut down. It was like I had been fighting against myself because my rational side knew damn well how great I had it at Google. If I had been meant to be behind a desk, I could have stayed at Google forever, but that tiny fire inside me was still burning. You know Billy Joel's song "Piano Man?" I'd second guess my life every time I heard those lyrics.

He said Bill I believe this is killing me/as the smile ran away from his face/well I'm sure that I could be a movie star/if I could get out of this place

For this reason, Google has been known as the "golden handcuffs." I knew what I had to do, but I just couldn't bring myself to do it. My best friends were at Google. The situation was fantastic. The offsite social events to ballgames and happy hours were almost too good to be true. And my savings account. Ah, my savings account.

Google was an absolutely incredible company to work for and I am so thankful for my experiences there. On top of the fun experiences and amazing opportunities (like Alpha testing the original Android software), my coworkers were incredible. We would brainstorm ways to change the world in our respective job areas and then meet up on breaks to play Guitar Hero. We'd have lunch overlooking the Bay Bridge and then have a conversation with a global company about how to improve their ROI. One of my coworkers, Jennica, and I are still best friends and we had the best time as teammates, doing fun things in the city, and forcing each other to use the vacation time that we constantly had saved up.

Jennica is that chick who is empathetic, kind, and really freaking fun. Whenever something good happens in my life, her excitement for me is genuine and, whenever something sucks, she will listen to me talk through it for way too long without telling me to shut up. My hope for every woman is to have a Jennica in their lives.

When I was considering leaving Google, the only thing I ever had to go on was my instinct, and that little voice inside of me that told me that while it was beyond great, for me it just wasn't….*it*. The entertainment industry was, which I'd known my whole life but hadn't been ready to fully accept. I wasn't built for instability and stress, and trying to make it in entertainment is peak levels of both - and the probability you'll fail is not only significant, you'll probably do it in the public eye more than once.

What I learned was that sometimes, you don't really have a choice. You see, I thought about it, and I thought about it, and I thought about it. Until one day, as you're about to find out, the decision was made for me.

TEN

The Skiing Incident

I woke up in Tahoe on a Sunday in March, much like I'd done on many previous ski season weekends. I got up, ate breakfast, packed a bag of snacks and headed off to Heavenly to be one of the first to enjoy the two feet of fresh powder that covered the mountain.

Heavenly Mountain has two sides: the Nevada side and the California side. My friends and I usually preferred to go up the Nevada side, up the Stagecoach Express chairlift and then venture out from there. Today was no different, as we parked at the Stagecoach Lodge and headed up to what we knew weather and scheduling wise could very well be the last day of our season.

Because it was late in the season and we'd gotten on the lift as soon as it opened, it seemed as though we were the only two people on the mountain. We were enjoying the quiet and crossing over to the lift that would bring us to the California side when my life changed forever.

I'd never skied in powder before. I was pretty comfortable on just about any groomed run but I didn't have powder-friendly skis and I was a total newbie in the powder department. Either way, I didn't think twice about launching down the hill toward the chairlift through the two feet of powder because, well, what could go wrong? Worst case scenario, I thought, you fall into a cloud and get a little snow in your jacket.

What happened next is somewhat of a blur.

About halfway down the run, my ski got stuck in the powder and angled downward, halting my projection immediately. As I fell forward, the stuck ski then pulled me back, at which point my ski snapped off of my binding. My ski and my head met somewhere in the middle, and I passed out.

I was only out for a short time, short enough to sit up disoriented and not realize what had happened. My ski buddy was waiting at the lift below, but it had happened so fast and he was far enough away that he wasn't sure what was happening other than that I didn't get up right away.

Dazed, I shoved my ski back on my binding and slowly made my way down to him. Everything was quiet, and there was still not a soul in sight. Actress Natasha Richardson, Liam Neeson's wife, had just died the week before after taking a small fall on a bunny hill, suffering an epidural hematoma. That's all I could think about as I said that I just needed to get checked out and then I was ready to keep skiing (it wasn't even 9 a.m. at this point). I insisted that I was fine to head down on my own and that we didn't need to radio for a medic.

Slowly, we made our way down the mountain.

As we got back to the lodge, someone went to get a medic for me. I remember sitting on a bench, facing what may have been a row of lockers, and feeling like I couldn't understand anything that was going on around me. I took my hat off and put my head between my legs in an effort to combat the dizziness, placing both hands on the back of my head as I did so. As my hands landed on my head, I realized that my hair was all matted and something didn't feel right.

In one motion I sat up and brought both of hands in front of my face, and couldn't totally process why my hands were covered in blood. The reality was that the ski had sliced the back of my head open, about an inch and a half above my spinal cord. That's probably when I went into shock. I do remember, as we waited for the ambulance, the medic telling me that I had one job. That job was to remember the phrase "purple flower, seven petals." I did my best to repeat it over and over in my head, unaware of anything else that was happening around me. I don't remember getting into the ambulance or leaving the mountain.

I do remember the EMTs talking to me with a very calm, gentle tone. They asked me if I'd ever ridden in an ambulance before (I hadn't) and tried to keep the conversation as normal as possible as we made our way to the hospital. It was almost like they were talking to a small child, though not in a condescending kind of way.

They knew I had a concussion of some sort, and tried to keep me awake both in the ambulance and at the hospital. I don't think I even felt the staples going into my head, but I did appreciate the nickname "FrankenSteph" that I was later given.

I got a CAT scan and the staples, and was finally allowed to rest. The next thing I really remember was part of the drive home from Tahoe to San Francisco. It was about a four-hour drive, and the one thing I wanted was a butterscotch-dipped ice cream cone from Dairy Queen.

An ice cream cone was always what we got as kids after a doctor's office visit. If we had to get a shot or something, we'd stay focused on the McDonald's run that would inevitably happen afterward. Now that I think about it, the positive reinforcement I got in those times is probably partly to blame for my ice cream addiction. I love ice cream. I could (and sometimes do) eat ice cream in some form every single day. YOLO.

On that note, I was completely focused on getting that ice cream cone. I was craving it, maybe because subconsciously I felt like I was owed it after what had happened. We pulled up to the drive-thru window and ordered the one thing I wanted more than anything else in the world at that moment. "We'll just take a small butterscotch dip cone, please."

With no hesitation, a voice with very little emotion came over the speaker and said, "We don't serve butterscotch dips at this location."

My eyes got wide and, with no words spoken, I immediately burst into tears.

There we sat in the Dairy Queen drive-thru while I cried and was unable to fathom what was happening to me at the moment. My thoughts were all over the place, my body was exhausted and now, worst of all, there would be no butterscotch ice cream. I was gently asked if I wanted a plain ice cream cone and after some hesitation I shrugged my shoulders through my tears.

The plain ice cream tasted terrible. Terrible! The ice cream itself wasn't inherently disgusting, but the plain without the butterscotch tasted completely different than the idea I'd had in my banged-up brain and, after one pathetic, tear-soaked lick I couldn't eat anymore.

We sat for a few minutes, and after getting it out of me that I thought McDonald's plain ice cream was far superior to Dairy Queen's plain ice cream, we went through McDonald's drive-thru and I took a breath and ate my cone as if it was my silver medal for my accomplishments. Not quite the gold, but still pretty good.

Getting back to San Francisco was the beginning of a wild year. I came back to my 150-square-foot studio that I'd just moved into. It was a tiny box, with the kitchen in the living room and just enough closet space to jam in my now three million pair of shoes. It was the first apartment I'd ever had without roommates, and I'd signed the rental agreement thinking the size wouldn't be an issue since I'd rarely be there.

Most of my time had previously been spent at the Google offices, at the gym or at some engagement around the city, and I was just happy to be in a position to afford San Francisco's insane rent on my own, even if it had one pull up window and the ugliest dark blue carpet that I'd ever seen for $1,400 a month. It was my space, and only mine. It also had a parking spot which to me was better than a functioning kitchen or any real airflow. The only problem was, I'd been completely sidelined and the cabin fever was real.

The first night that I lay down in this apartment after it had all gone down was also the first night in my life that I'd ever experienced true insomnia. I was more exhausted than I could ever remember being, and all I wanted to do was doze off and forget the world for a while. I had staples in my head, an injured neck, and had been everywhere from an emergency room in Tahoe to my primary care doctor's office in Menlo Park in the previous days and nothing sounded better than crawling into my bed, curling up with Fifi and sleeping it all away.

The feeling of lying there when your body is at peak exhaustion but your mind has other plans is almost indescribable. It's like everything from your brain to your chest is wide awake, your thoughts are either racing or just taking full advantage of the silence, and your body is screaming back "Shut the hell up and let me sleep!" After a few nights of this, my doctor prescribed me Xanax, which was the only way I got any rest.

On top of some muscle injuries in my neck and back that required physical therapy, I had moments where I'd be convinced that those around me were speaking in foreign languages, and I was so paranoid when I'd walk alone that I would constantly be checking over my shoulder.

I'd hold my key ring in my pocket, tightly clutched between my two first fingers in a way that if anyone was there when I turned around, I could hopefully swing and use my keys as a weapon. There's obviously very little damage that could be done that way and someone later showed me how a key between my first two fingers may have been more practical, but it was the only way I felt okay being in one of the safest neighborhoods in the city.

I went on medical leave from Google, and would end up rehabbing both physically and mentally for almost a year. I knew that whatever happened after this, my life would never be the same - not necessarily when it came to my mental or physical health, but instead my path in life and the decisions that I made.

At first, trying to read and respond to emails was nearly impossible. I could read each word individually and I was aware that I knew the words on my screen, but I couldn't process what the email was saying nor could I formulate a proper response no matter how hard I tried. I hadn't lost the ability to read, but the ability to process what I was reading.

At some point, I was given the book "Twilight" as it had been suggested that I take an easy read and try and fight my way through it. It took me days to get through even the first page. I read it over and over again, not processing any of it. But slowly, word by word, it came back, and when it came back it was a fast curve. I think the concussion had a lot to do with issues like this, but I also think I was also completely overwhelmed with trying to process all of the chaos that my body and brain were experiencing.

After a few months, I went through hours of psychological testing at Stanford and was told that I tested in the 16th percentile for my age, demographic and educational background. That was terrifying. By this point I was starting to feel like a functioning human again on some levels, but my response times were slow, my ability to process still needed work and I was an anxious, emotional mess most of the time.

Over time (I was on leave from Google for approximately 10 months) and with help, I started to feel like myself again. No effects from that day were permanent or still linger to this day, with the exception of tight neck and shoulder muscles and the occasional feeling like I'm underwater or in a pressurized plane. Toward the end of my leave, my biggest struggle was still just processing what had happened. I'd sit in my tiny San Francisco apartment all day with Fifi and try to stay sane and figure out my next move.

Though I didn't consider myself to be religious at the time, I look back at this period and think that God knew that I was going to have a hard time ever leaving Google, even though my heart was elsewhere. I really believe He made some moves to nudge me in the right direction. When I was on camera or on stage, I was a different person, and I'd wanted to be on TV since I was a kid. My dad tells the story of how we went to the movie theater once when I was really young and I walked up to the screen and said "Dad, I want to be in there with the toys."

That being said, I seemingly had it all at Google. Stability, stock options, medical benefits, great friends. Making the decision to leave that and be self-employed, hoping that my dreams in life wouldn't lead me into a dark alley of sadness and an empty bank account, was one of the hardest things I've ever had to do.

After rehabbing and navigating one of the strangest times in my life, the same week that I'd been medically cleared to return to Google my agency called and told me that I had an audition lined up for an ambiguous sounding project. A tech company was looking for a spokesperson, and it was a very simple audition that I wrote off almost immediately, considering it went, in part, something like this:

Casting Lady: What is your current ringtone?
Me: Great question - my phone is on vibrate 90 percent of the time, but I'm happy to check for you...
Casting Lady: (laughs) no, that's okay.

The whole thing took maybe three minutes. Who knows what exactly they were looking for, but I got a callback audition in which I spent more time talking about myself, what I use my phone for the most, and my life in tech.

It started to look like a real possibility, but Google also needed to know if I'd be coming back. I badgered my agent for weeks, but the only answer I got was that they had nothing set in stone, but that it seemed like good news.

The waiting game was torturous. Every day I'd wake up and check my email, and then refresh every 15 minutes. And each day that went by without an email left me feeling more and more defeated.

Pretty soon, I had no choice. I had to pray to God that my instincts were right, and, with no guarantees whatsoever, I quit the best job I'd ever had. A job that paid well, that taught me irreplaceable lessons, and that allowed me to live in a city with one of the highest costs of living in the world.

In total, five months went by after the initial audition. I started to brainstorm other ways to make money in case my financial situation went to shit (I did, in fact, have to cash out my 401(k) early). I also tried everything to not go insane when my agent would tell me, every week upon my check-in email, that there was no news. I started to absolutely panic and given that the high-stress insomniac that I already was, it wasn't pretty.

As it goes, just as I was starting to think every penny I'd made at Google would be out the window, my agent excitedly called and said they'd received a contractual offer.

They wanted me to be The LG Girl, the face and voice of everything LG Mobile. My head was spinning. Here it was, after months of waiting - an equal mix of smart, technological topics and the ability to write and be on camera in the creative space.

What I learned during this year of my life is that no matter how stable your life may seem, anything can be taken away from you in an instant. I was lucky, or blessed, or however you want to look at it – but walking away from an injury that was a quarter of an inch from your spinal cord is a real wake-up call.

I also realized that just because something is really, really good, doesn't mean that it's what you should spend your life doing. It took me a few months of of stress followed by a year being sidelined to get the guts to venture into entertainment, and while it seems like such wasted time, that was my path.

I *loved* Google. I really did. I made amazing friends there and the workplace environment was unlike anything else. But toward the end of my time there, there was always something urging me to not lose sight of what I'd wanted to do in my life since birth. The anxiety and stress of making a major life change in your late 20s is real and significant. But, if you're making that decision because you're following your heart, it's not only the right decision, but, one way or another, things will almost always fall into place.

What I learned is that sometimes, it takes a giant event like a ski accident to give you what *Psychology Today* calls an "aha, life changing moment." But sometimes, really listening to yourself is all you need. I fully believe in gut instinct. We inherently know what's right and wrong for ourselves, but only occasionally do we have the guts to listen.

Ask yourself this: Do I want to be at this company, or in this relationship, or doing whatever it is that I'm doing in 10 years? If so, what would that look like? And if not, well...you may have some big decisions to make. And it's going to be hard, and stressful, and scary. Like Phoebe tells Ross after Rachel has Emma, "I know, I know.

And if you try to make it more, you might wreck it. Or, you might get everything you've wanted since you were 15." Spoiler alert - in the end, he gets everything he wanted since he was 15.

ELEVEN

Paid Actress

I've always been one to learn things the hard way, or at the very least learn things on my own. It's who I am. Problem is, there is no way of learning when you have no one/nothing there to guide you, and there are so many things I wish that I had known before leaving the corporate world and becoming Stephanie Duchaine, LLC. Okay, there's no LLC. But I should probably look into that because I feel like there should be an LLC, or at least something like it. Almost a decade later and I still don't totally understand all of the necessities but hey, I'm doing okay.

In any situation, it's of course always helpful if you have someone to guide you or at least someone that you can go to with questions who has been there before. I didn't have anyone like that in my life when I ventured into the self-employment world and, frankly, I didn't even think about it. Everyone close to me had been working at the same company for most of their adult lives and they all still had 401(k)s and health benefits and I had no reason to believe that my life would be any different. It's kind of like when I went to Amsterdam and just assumed that they spoke English - let's just say that in recent years I've started aggressively researching *everything*. Google is my friend.

I love learning and I love expanding my horizons, and I very much make decisions and moves based on an educated instinct. If I want something, it might take me a long-ass time to make the leap, but, eventually, I go get it regardless of the hurdles that I may have to jump through, a life lesson that I learned from my dad. He would tell all of us, on numerous occasions, that if there is something that needs to be accomplished you need to "do what you need to do to get the job done." Figuring out how to do it the right way. Getting creative. Working overtime. Whatever.

On this path, I find myself making the decisions that I feel are right and then fighting through the outcome when it wasn't what I expected (and it never really was). Trust me, nothing ever looks like you thought it would, and any sort of pretty life plans that you had were more than likely just wishful thinking. It took me 30 full years to be able to accept that fact and even try to just go with the flow, and it's still a process to make myself relax.

Let's start with working as The LG Girl. I'd been contracted by an advertising agency to become the face and voice of a global brand, and I loved every minute of the work that I was hired to do. I traveled the country, hosted red carpets and events, and created a series of First Look videos that got over a million views on YouTube.

I was qualified for that job because I'd had some performing experience in the theater, but also because I genuinely loved and knew about technology and especially mobile devices. I felt great about why I was hired - until I started reading tweets and YouTube comments.

One of my all-time favorite comments was on one of my first videos (a video that I'd written, shot, edited and published), about a top-of-the-line smart phone that was just released. The comment said I was clearly a "paid actress" and told LG that they needed to start hiring people who knew what they were talking about. I've been called ugly, told to get back in the kitchen, or sexualized more times that you can count and, whether it's a good thing or a bad thing, I'm completely desensitized to it.

I had to, pretty quickly, get over the initial shock of what people will say to you behind a keyboard. I learned that being in the public eye means you're going to be criticized no matter what, and the comments can be outrageous. Beyond that, being a woman who works primarily in technology, I always knew I was going to have to work very hard to be taken seriously as a credible technology analyst, commentator or reporter. I'd have to work even harder to do what I really wanted to do, which was make technology relatable and give my opinions on it.

That being said, I have not yet adapted to tuning out things people say about my boyfriend, Mike. He's currently a pitcher for the Chicago Cubs, and after he pitched in game four against the Nationals in the 2017 NLDS (which they lost), he got tweets telling him that he should go die. It took everything in me (especially after I'd had a few beers) to not lose my shit.

The thing is, for every bad comment, there are many good ones. People can be cruel, but they can also be really, really great. There were some people who had reputable tech blogs or were reputable developers that did not, though they could have, treat me with any disrespect. I'm fully aware that I don't look or maybe even present myself like I work in technology, but with the support of people who were only focused on improving the world of tech, I buckled down and kept doing my thing.

Thanks to some open-minded dudes, I was able to start a conversation between myself (on behalf of a smartphone manufacturer) and the developer community. A conversation that was unusual and uncommon, started between the brilliant minds that create independent applications and the manufacturer of the phones. It wasn't easy for them to send feedback to a global corporation (it's nearly impossible to get the contact for the appropriate person to talk to, and actually have them respond), and for whatever small role I played in having their voices heard, I am happy that I could do that.

On a beautiful day in the spring, just after signing on with LG, the digital agency that I was working with wanted to shoot an introductory video called "A Day in the Likes." The goal of this video was to introduce myself to people in the social space while showcasing some fun technology around the city of San Francisco, as well as different things that I liked. At this point, I was on cloud 9 – I was working as a contracted host and writer and I was about to get paid to go film a video around one of my favorite cities in the world.

I had also just moved into my dream San Francisco apartment, which is where we started the shoot. It was a one-bedroom third-floor walkup, with beautiful bay windows that overlooked Hyde Street. I was right on the cable car line and I loved sitting in the window and watching it go by beneath the trees that lined my view. There was no garbage disposal or dishwasher, but it had wood floors and a walk-in closet, with glass French doors that separated the bedroom from the living room. Last I heard, they'd turned the building into a condo complex and tripled the rent.

All right, so this "A Day in the Likes" video. It was a play on Facebook likes, given that the video would be the introduction to my Facebook fan page for The LG Girl. Weird, but exciting. We went to a vet with Fifi and talked about microchips, and then went to a specialized fitness studio where I interviewed the owner about the high-altitude chamber while running on a treadmill within it. We then headed down to Pier 39 to begin the last part of the shoot.

We were going to embark on a Segway tour, and I'd be rolling around with my own personal guide while the camera followed me. I'd be learning about how these things worked and I'd talk about how great this method of transportation was.

It all started smoothly enough, until the last shot of the day. At that point everyone knew how much I loved ice cream and we had the following idea to shoot as b-roll: The camera would stay in one place, and I'd zip by first holding an ice cream cone, then come the other way with cotton candy, and finally, a giant soft pretzel.

As I heard "Action!" I'd forgotten that, many years ago, I'd proven to myself that I should not be allowed on a scooter or anything like it as I looked into the camera, smiled, and went to take my first bite of a giant Ben and Jerry's cookie dough ice cream cone. It was exactly the shot we'd wanted to get, until I hit a bench and went flying as tourists from around the world let out a collective gasp. Even better was the fact that, in the shot before, I could be seen saying straight to the camera that "I've been riding the Segway around for a little while and I have to say that while I am normally a huge klutz, but I've managed to not fall off – which I think says a lot about the safety of this thing." This is a true story and if you Google "Segway Crash Raw Footage" you can see it for yourself.

My helmet hadn't been buckled tightly and I had a massive bruise on my hip. I actually wasn't embarrassed. In fact, in all seriousness I remember rolling over and looking at the pigeons descending on the ice cream cone and feeling so defeated. I'm depressed just thinking about it. The crew rushed over to help me up and, once they made sure that I was okay, the camera man gave me an uneasy laugh as he asked me if I had good medical insurance.

Oh right...*medical insurance*. One of the things I gave up when I left Google. Luckily my hip was just a bruise and felt much better after I took the night off to rest, watch *Law and Order: SVU* reruns and make myself some "sorry about the ice cream" funfetti cupcakes. I may have had a mild concussion, but I was really freakin' lucky that's all it was, especially after the last year of my life. I don't know what I was thinking getting on a Segway to begin with, much less without medical insurance.

The next big "I work for myself" shock came during tax season the following year. When you're self-employed, no one withholds tax for you throughout the year. So not only are you expected to pay estimated tax every quarter, but you're also responsible for paying a good chunk of money out of pocket (including a self-employment tax) to cover things like Social Security. Who knew? Not me. After almost 10 years of every job I'd ever had taking taxes out for me and usually being owed a refund, imagine my surprise when I found out that I had to write the IRS a check that cleared out my entire savings account. Everything I'd worked for was, once again, gone.

I got very, very lucky in that, when I ventured into self-employment and took the first step to following my dreams, I still had a safety net. Even after I emptied my savings account, I had renewed my contract with LG and I knew there would be more paychecks coming in. When I fell off the Segway, my injury was just enough to push me to sign up for health insurance ASAP, but not enough to cause any real damage.

The hardest part of all of this was feeling like I didn't know anything, and that I was starting over at 27 years of age. I was navigating a new industry and, while I was confident in my performing and technology skills, the truth is that I was a newbie.

When learning any new trade, there are an insane amount of things that you don't know and not mentioning one thing by its correct name can out you as an amateur, real quick. There are an incredible amount of ways to make yourself look stupid, to fail or to not be taken seriously. The amount of Hollywood lingo I had to learn to make myself credible was extensive. So, for the first few years, it was just about keeping my mouth shut, keeping my questions direct but ambiguous and listening as much as possible.

What I learned is that if the fear of failing or "starting over" is what's holding you back from taking the leap into the career you're dying to be in, you should, most certainly, take the leap. Fear is nothing but unwarranted worry about something that may not ever even happen.

TWELVE

Small Fish, Big Pond

When I was working in the entertainment industry in San Francisco, I became, to some degree, a big fish in a small pond. I shot a few commercials here and there and then booked The LG Girl, which took me around the country covering events, blogging on behalf of the company and shooting videos that documented my adventures.

I ended up hitting a bit of a ceiling, as I got to a point where thanks to LG I had a significant following in the tech space and, because of contractual agreements, there was no additional tech hosting or commercial work that I could do in the Bay Area.

When you're a host or an actress, you're usually free to work with many different clients, assuming they're not competitors and the shooting schedules don't overlap. When I first got the offer from LG, I knew I wouldn't be able to work for any competitors (like Samsung, for example) but I didn't dig any deeper into it.

Quite honestly, I signed that contract while giving minimal pushback. I wanted the security and the money, and given that it was my first contract of the sort, I also had no idea what questions to ask. That was a mistake that ended up biting me in the ass. When I signed it, I didn't know that there was an exclusivity agreement in my contract that forbid me from working with any telecommunications company (small print: anything that sent a signal. Basically anything tech, competitor of LG or not), which was a huge part of the San Francisco market. Because of this, I missed out on experience, exposure and a significant amount of money - which, as you'll see, is vital to pad the ol' savings account for the inevitable downswings of self-employment in the entertainment industry.

It became pretty clear that if I really wanted to go on with this on-camera thing, it was time to branch out of the niche northern market and move to Los Angeles. The lease on my apartment was up and, while I could afford it, I started the moving process. I figured that I had enough experience under my belt to be able to confidently enter the wider entertainment world, and, having been the face of a global company, I figured my credibility would speak for itself.

I'd only been to Los Angeles a few times before, mainly on short vacations with my family. One visit when I was 17, however, was arguably the most significant in that it was my first experience with what this business looked like. Let's rewind.

My mother is her children's biggest fan, no matter what we do. She still encourages me to "sing and dance in auditions" because I am "very talented" in that realm. I can not express to you how badly I wish there was a way to translate my singing skills onto the page. My only redeeming vocal quality is that I can match a note pretty well, but my voice is never going to soothe you to sleep. My mother is my biggest cheerleader on all levels, that is an indisputable fact.

In one of her "talk me up" conversations, she told a family friend that I wanted to be an actress, and he mentioned that he would be more than willing to put me in touch with a friend of his who was a casting director. A very sweet gesture. Thank you, Paul.

This was before the days where everything was digital, so I actually had to call her *home phone*. As I mentioned, I was 17 at the time and beneath my fake confident attitude I was really just an insecure, 90-pound shrimp who wore weird clothes like jeans with sparkles on them and big platform heeled boots. The realization that I had a connection that could potentially determine if I was actually meant to be an actress was terrifying. It took me a very long time to make that call but, once I did, as my voice shook, a no-nonsense woman agreed to set up an appointment at her office down in the motherland. She asked me to come prepared to read a Shakespearean monologue. My father put together the details of the travel, and off we went.

I'm cringing as I write this: I chose Hamlet's "to be, or not to be" monologue. There are so many problems with this, I don't even know where to begin. Regardless of the fact that Hamlet is a grown-ass man, I'd never ventured outside of community theater nor had I paid any attention in class when we'd study such literature. So it was essentially like I was memorizing a foreign language and hoping that it translated well when the words came out of my mouth. I'd always had a good memory, so that part wasn't too bad, and I started to figure that maybe memorizing stuff and repeating it was just what people did in Los Angeles.

It was horrible. Absolutely horrible. She stopped me not long after I started and said that the first thing that she wanted me to know was that if someone asked me to read Shakespeare and I didn't know how to read Shakespeare, that I needed to say that.

She was either being nice because of the family friend connection or she did actually see something in me that glimmered through my horrendous reading, but she said that she would be willing to work with me - but that there was nothing that she could do until I moved to Los Angeles. Because of how quickly I move in my life, I made sure to promptly move to Los Angeles 10 years later, after she'd left the casting business. I'd blown that connection, but I had never forgotten the experience.

Before moving to L.A., I lived in four different cities and seven different homes/apartments. By the time I moved I considered myself to be easily adaptable, and I'd gotten quite used to moving around and going with the flow when it came to learning a new city.

Let me tell you, L.A. is unlike anything I'd ever seen before. To begin, the traffic is as bad as everyone says it is. When I first came down to scope things out, I was staying with my sister in Santa Monica and I had an audition in West Hollywood at one o'clock in the afternoon. It took me over an hour to travel eight miles, and the same amount of time to get home.

I learned very quickly that having an agent in and of itself can mean very little in terms of finding new opportunities. They will put you out there when they can, but you are still largely responsible for building your own career, keeping your materials (reel, website, whatever) up to date, and doing what you need to do to get yourself out there.

I signed with one of the biggest agencies in the country before I moved, and thought I was set - but upon landing in Los Angeles, very quickly realized that when you're a host, the auditions aren't a dime a dozen. In fact, one audition a month is pretty good. I also realized that any previous success you may have found means nothing.

You see, hosting falls under the "unscripted and alternative programming" umbrella, which is also where reality TV lies, and there are significantly more opportunities to be a reality star than there are to host your own show. Or to host anything, for that matter, especially since I was a very specific kind of "talent": not a journalist, not the sexy co-host in the miniskirt, just someone who loved being on camera and wanted to talk about smart content. I'd done it with mobile phones, so would finding the next project really be that difficult? It was, actually.

For a while, I thought that every audition was going to be the biggest day of my life, especially when the auditions weren't coming around as often as I would have liked and my savings account was dwindling at an alarming rate. I'd get an audition for a big project and I'd get so in my head about it that, by the time the audition rolled around, I couldn't even think straight. My mind would be racing about how I better not blow this, because *this* would be my big break and *this* would be absolutely perfect for me and my bank account would be replenished.

By the time I walked in the room I was happy if I remembered what I was supposed to say and didn't pass out. I was devastated after just about every single one, feeling like I just blew my potential big break.

Little did I know that 99 percent of the shows that I auditioned for wouldn't make it past their first season, assuming they aired at all. This is how it works in this business, as everyone wants to create the next big thing and it's a continual process on every level, from the actor to the studio and the audition to the pilot, to find that one needle in the Hollywood haystack.

After almost a year on the hamster wheel, there were so many nights that I spent beating my head into the wall wondering why nothing was happening, wondering what was wrong with me and how I was going to pay my rent. My collegiate workflow mindset of "work hard and good things will happen" was failing me, as it seemed that I could no longer guarantee that if I worked hard, I'd find success in the same way that I had gotten good grades or a promotion. I also couldn't stop comparing myself to other people, which was insanely destructive.

There are a lot of people in this industry who do questionable things. Things that I don't understand or agree with, from cheating on their significant others like it didn't matter in the slightest to staying up all night in a coke-fueled rage, and I'd look at them and wonder how they had so many followers on Twitter or how they had been cast as the lead in a movie. I'd analyze every single thing that I could possibly analyze in an effort to figure out what I was doing wrong. I knew that I wasn't willing to compromise on my morals and beliefs, but it began to seem like doing so was the only way to make a name for yourself.

When you love something and you're constantly rejected despite your continual grind, your mind starts to inevitably wonder if it's time to cut the cord. There was one time where I had a meeting in New York City, and the day before, the guy I was supposed to meet with went completely MIA. With me, anyway. He was still very active on social media, so I knew he was alive. For whatever reason, after weeks of communication, he decided he didn't really feel like meeting anymore. I flew back to L.A., got the flu, and spent a week in bed wanting to scream but being physically unable to move. That was a new level of defeat.

Years later, he added me on LinkedIn, which I was super confused about - until I saw that his banner image was of the Cubs winning the World Series. The same World Series where my now boyfriend threw the last pitch. Save it, moron.

As you know by now, I'm a studier. I research everything. If I don't understand something, I like to read about it, from personality tests and sports statistics to the journeys of others. If I admire someone's career, I read their Wikipedia page to get an understanding of how they got to where they are.

I read a lot of interviews, and I eventually discovered one common thread among people who have achieved great success. The one thought that everyone I admired seemed to share was that they refused to stay down during times of adversity. Ask successful people why they're successful, and they'll tell you because they've fallen down hundreds of times, and no matter how hard it is, they always get back up.

I can not stress how true this is. After a year or two of hitting every single wall that I could hit, I was running on fumes. My savings account was almost gone, I had no motivation, and I was constantly thinking about how I just might not be able to cut it. There were (many) days where I didn't leave my apartment at all, moping around in a depressed state thinking about how much I hated the industry I'd chosen. I had a college degree, I was a former Google employee and damn it, I was just the face of a global brand! Why was I suddenly borderline broke and jobless?

Just as I'd start to think that maybe I couldn't cut it and I'd wonder if my rent was going to be late, I'd book a small job that would remind me how alive I felt when I was in front of the camera and creating content. The slightest taste of that was enough to remind me why I needed to keep going.

That's the thing about industries like this. I assume that it's the same with just about any competitive or creative career: You will inevitably come to a crossroads, and, if you decide to move forward, you better make damn sure that you love what you're doing so deeply that pursuing it professionally is what you're prepared to do no matter what ups and downs come at you. If you don't love it at the deepest level of your soul, you'll never make it.

If you do love it, though, you'll find that no matter how down in the dumps you feel, things will eventually happen. I know that probably seems like such easy advice to give, and impossible advice to take. Realistically, if anyone would have given me that advice when I was paying my bills on my credit card and crying myself to sleep at night I would have told them to shove that advice up their ass - and the only reason I believe it now is because I've lived it. I've been $10,000 in debt and I've bet everything on myself. Money, time, emotional sanity, you name it. And only after three years in Los Angeles did it pay off.

I was sitting in my apartment one day when my San Francisco agency, who I rarely worked with anymore, emailed me to ask my available for a trade show in Vegas. The amount of money they were going to pay me was more than I'd made in the last year, but they liked my hosting reel (made up mostly of LG videos that were then 3 years old) and my website. They asked me to do a self-taped audition, which was rare, and I booked the job. Another thing to file under the *how-the-hell-was-that-possible* label.

My comeback didn't end there. While I was in Vegas, I got an email through my website - the same website that I'd built years earlier - asking me if I would be interested in potentially partnering with the Home Shopping Network. They said they were interested in branching out with their digital programming, and came across my website when looking for female talent who were knowledgeable about tech. I told them I was definitely interested, but was working another job in Vegas so my audition tape would have to be sent from my hotel room on my break.

Are you kidding me? I hadn't worked in months, and yet here I was, able to sound so important. Like yes, Home Shopping Network, I *may* be able to fit you in in, but you caught me at a busy time.

They liked my audition tape. I booked a digital series. And right before I was set to fly out, they asked me if I wanted to try out a live show while I was there.

Are you convinced, yet? What in the world are the chances that after years of rejections, I'd not only book one high-paying job, but I'd also book a second high paying job in the middle of working that first job?

After the Vegas trade show hosting, I flew to Tampa for my trial with HSN. It went well and I not only ended up with my own series called "The Hot Spot," but I was also a guest on countless live shows on HSN for more than two years.

The personal growth that I felt from age 28 to age 30 was unlike any other years of my life. It took me a long time to figure out that having a college degree meant literally nothing to most people in Los Angeles casting rooms, and that I was merely one of one million brunette women who wanted to "make it." I spent so much time having no freaking idea what was coming next. This was extremely difficult for someone who had gotten into the mindset and work ethic of "study hard, get good grades" and "work hard, get promoted."

But that was the beautiful thing. Without the harsh realization that nothing was going to come easy, I wouldn't be the tough bitch that I am today (only in entertainment. I'm still incredibly soft emotionally). I learned that sometimes the only path is one of determination, faith, perseverance and the willingness to keep moving forward, no matter what.

I had always thought that the path to success in this business was to audition until you're blue in the face, and then audition some more and, eventually, something would happen. Let me tell you, to this day I haven't booked one significant job from an audition. I booked smaller roles and one-off jobs, but every single long-term contractual position that I've booked after I moved to Los Angeles has nothing to do with any audition that I've ever gone on. Most of them occurred because the clients had come across my website that I'd built years earlier. To this day, they're some of the greatest clients that I've worked with.

What I learned in that stretch of time when I was paying my rent on a credit card advance, doing everything that I could to find my footing with no guarantee of success (after I'd had true, stable success at Google) was a real lesson in picking yourself back up every single time you're knocked down. You will be knocked down, sometimes with no clear view of how you'll ever get back up, but with a little bit of faith and an attitude of perseverance, the excitement of the journey can be greater than the stress of the unknown.

THIRTEEN

Fake It 'Til You Make It

I consider myself to be pretty tough. I'm independent, stubborn, and self-sufficient and I've learned a lot of lessons the hard way, which has built up some thick skin as well as an arsenal of tools to help me push forward on new endeavors. Let's not get it twisted, though - as I mentioned in the last chapter, I am emotional as f.

The breakdown goes something like this. You can call me names and it doesn't affect my self-worth. You can tell me the harsh truth, and I appreciate it because then I know what I'm working with. You can bullshit me when it comes to my career and I'll get pissed or roll my eyes.

That being said, if something touches me, whether I'm in church, watching a movie, or listening to an emotional story, I'll tear up. If something significant happens to someone I love, good or bad, I'm crying.

At first, it was a process to manage my emotions. If I felt it, you'd know it. If I was pissed, I'd snap. If I was sad, I'd cry. And if I was over it, I'd make sure you knew I was over it and I'd be gone before you knew it. Then, somewhere along the line, I started to grow up and learn the art of being stoic.

There was one moment in recent history when I realized that I was truly an adult, and it became clear that sometimes you need to (wo)man up and handle your business, no matter what is happening around you. After a few years of brick walls and dead ends, I was working consistently again after the Home Shopping Network reached out to me via by website to ask if I'd be interested in collaborating. Quite honestly, I only fully appreciated this opportunity to be on camera in front of millions of people because I'd been rejected so much in the years prior. I felt like I really had earned it.

After traveling to Tampa once a month for HSN in the previous year, I was back in Florida for some live TV spots talking about the latest and greatest in the world technology. The network had brought me on as the "resident tech gal" where I would both shoot a digital series focused on tech tips and act as a guest during the live shows, talking about how I used individual technologies and gadgets to make my life better.

It was a Saturday, and I was scheduled to be on-air for numerous live TV spots, being broadcast to millions of homes around the country, between 9 a.m. and 10 p.m. EST. I was so happy and grateful to be there, but, as it happens in life, there were a few things happening that were bringing me down.

First of all, my family had been struggling with the fact that my Aunt Tammi wasn't going to be with us much longer. There are no amount of words to describe what she meant to me, but she was beyond special. She was so endlessly proud of me that, to this day, I joke about how I could have been on TV talking about something so far from glamorous, like tampons, and she would have told all of her friends to tune in and then raved about how amazing I was at making feminine hygiene relatable.

That morning, I'd called my father on my way to my green room as I knew that it was also very touch and and go with our family dog, Blue, who was suffering from an aggressive form of bone cancer. I dried the tears of hearing my father choked up just as it was time to hit the makeup chair and knock out the morning shows. My dad called me back a few hours later from the vet's office, our family conferenced in from Florida, Seattle, and Los Angeles as we said a prayer, bawled our eyes out and said goodbye to our faithful family pup.

An hour later, I was back on television smiling through my stage makeup doing my absolute best to provide absolutely no indication that anything had happened during the break between shows or had been happening for weeks before. It was on this day, six years into my professional television career, that I truly gave myself credit for being a professional.

Entertainment is a funny thing. We've all heard the phrase "the show must go on" and, no matter what, *the show must go on*. Whether live or scripted, these projects have more pieces than you could ever imagine, from the budgets to the hired manpower. For me, showing up to every single shoot ready to go is non-negotiable. I love every minute of what I do, but being focused and flipping the switch whenever you're on set is a mental adjustment that you learn to develop and perfect each time you see the red recording light on the camera.

I'm in awe of Mike's ability to do this. Professional athletes don't have the luxury of letting life get in the way of their game. For baseball players, it doesn't matter if your kid (or dog) was up sick all night, if you're injured or not feeling well or if you're going through a divorce. For 162-plus days of the season, you're letting an entire team (and an entire fanbase) down if you don't go out there and perform.

Sometimes all you want to do is cry. The defeat and the pain feels overwhelming and you wonder how you can possibly handle all of the responsibilities and life events that lie before you. And while there is nothing wrong with taking some time to process, there's also something very powerful in being able to smile and function through the pain or the unknown. We've heard that phrase in so many ways: from "dress for success" to "fake it until you make it."

That day on camera was a day that I'll never forget. From sunup to well after sundown, I'd experienced numerous live TV spots, the death of our furry sibling and hearing my father cry (which has happened maybe twice in my life). By the time I crawled into my bed at the hotel, I was so numb and fatigued that I felt more like a zombie than a human being.

I had met my friend Becca while in her makeup chair months ago, and she and I immediately became inseparable. I usually have a hard time opening up to people right away, but, as Chris Isaak's "Wicked Games" came on her iPod while she made me look TV presentable, we bonded over what a jam that was and it was all uphill from there.

She and I had planned long before to drive out to Lakeland the next day to watch a Spring Training game. We sat, laughed, ate Red Vines and watched one of the slowest Spring Training games ever, spanning more than four hours. Though I hadn't slept in who knows how long, I found myself more at ease than I had been in weeks as Becca listened to my experience and I realized that I'd gotten through a very long professional day without anyone knowing the pain I was feeling or the tears I was crying. I learned that life happens. Death happens. And pain happens. But life doesn't stop and relying on God, family, career, or whatever it is that you need to rely on is what will get you through to the next day.

I'm not a big Social Sally, nor do I have a giant group of close friends that all get together. What I do have is an incredible support system and a small group of people that I can trust with anything, any time. Especially working in an industry of smoke and mirrors, I couldn't be more thankful.

There was an unexplainable calm and happiness that I felt that day with Becca amid all of the chaos, even as we sped back from Lakeland to the Tampa airport (about an hour with no traffic), cutting it closer than I ever had for a flight.

I had a 9:30 a.m. shoot the following morning in Burbank, and I was booked on the last flight out. I ran through the airport, making it from the curb to my seat in 18 minutes (thank you TSA precheck) just as the door closed - and after a short flight to Houston I sat during my layover en route to LAX sweating from my intense sunburn and feeling very accomplished and suddenly aware of a shift in maturity and professionalism.

What I learned is that everything that you experience is just another piece to your puzzle, and, with the right attitude and the right support system, you really can fake it 'til you make it through anything that may arise.

FOURTEEN

Over-Stimulation

I love coffee. At this point, my blood is likely part medium roast, part red wine.

After my routine Saturday morning circuit training workout, I usually get a latte because I've convinced myself that I need the protein to properly recover, but my go-to daily beverage is a straight cup of Starbucks black coffee. Breakfast Blend if I make it at home (usually) and Pike Place Roast if I go in store. No cream, no sugar, no nothing.

I'm a Starbucks girl for a few reasons. First, I'm from Seattle, home of the original Starbucks and land of a Starbucks on every corner. Second, I like it. It tastes good, and it's also good for my emotions in a hometown comfort kind of way. Finally, their coffee happens to have one of the highest caffeine levels on the market. Caffeine is great. I don't trust anyone who says they don't drink caffeine, and when someone tells me they don't drink coffee in particular, I'm always a little suspicious.

For a while, in the years after my skiing incident, I would start with a cup of coffee and then mid-afternoon have a shot or two of espresso. Again, straight up. I don't usually see any need of messing with a good thing by adding anything extra, unless you're adding hot water at which point your espresso becomes an Americano and the drinking experience lasts longer. The way I feel about adding cream and sugar to a cup of coffee is the same way I feel about adding a tomato slice to a great hamburger. Why would you take away from the experience like that?

The more coffee that I drank during that time, the more coffee I needed to feel functional. If I still felt sluggish after my espressos, I would tell myself I was being reasonable by drinking tea in the late afternoon, but then I'd then be so frustrated lying in my bed each night wondering why my "anxiety" was keeping me awake.

I put anxiety in quotes not because mine had gone away, but because it was an easy thing to blame my sleepless nights on. It had become a vicious cycle after the skiing accident: insomnia, feeling like a zombie during the day, drinking increasing amounts of coffee, insomnia. The only way that I could get any sleep was by taking one of the Xanax that my doctor had prescribed to me, which became a crutch. After a while, I was almost surely addicted on some level to both caffeine and to Xanax (even though tiny amounts were all I needed, I was taking one-eighth of a standard dose).

I had been so focused on the head injury and just accepting that anxiety was a part of my life that I lost sight of the other habits that were ruining my sleep patterns and keeping my heart racing. I only started to realize them when I got horrendously desperate after feeling like I hadn't slept normally in years, and started to research potential fixes on top of what I'd already tried, which included melatonin, over-the-counter sleep aids, and things of that sort.

Every day, each of us face more alerts and pressures than ever before. Think about all of the things that we're presented with on a daily basis, before we even consider interpersonal situations. Targeted ads that prompt us to buy those shoes that we were just looking at on Amazon. Ten new emails in the inbox before the sun has come up. Being exposed to so-and-so's new photo album on Facebook from her recent vacation with her husband and kids. And on top of all of this, we work to juggle family, friends, school, a fulfilling career, and sometimes, a social life.

After trying what feels like a million different things, I've found a few basics that have helped me. The first is limiting caffeine after noon. If I'm having an exceptionally long and tiring day, I might double up on the cups of coffee, but for the most part I try to go with my one highly caffeinated Starbucks beverage in the morning and call it a day. It's also interesting because caffeine creeps up in unexpected places – for a while I thought I was being healthy by having dark chocolate for dessert, but it turns out that caffeine is secretly in there, too. The darker the chocolate, the more caffeine. Who knew, right? There's obviously not as much as there would be in, say, a cup of coffee, but my body is sensitive enough to those kinds of things that I feel it.

The second is limiting myself to one glass of wine per night, which is a work in progress. I love a good glass of red and, for the most part, I'll admit that my wine tolerance is pretty high. That being said, numerous studies show that one glass helps sleep patterns, but any more than that and you're hurting your sleep cycle. I hate to say it, but it seems to be the truth. I've also read articles that a glass of wine equals an hour in the gym, and that red wine helps you live longer. So, it's for my health.

The third is working out vigorously. I started doing HIIT (high intensity training) and, assuming I don't take the evening classes, I've found myself sleeping so much better because my body is completely done afterwards. Shoutout to Basecamp Fitness and

OrangeTheory. They're the freakin' best. If you're new to circuit training, my suggestion is giving it three sessions before deciding if it's right for you, because I wanted to throw up and never go back after my first class. It's *hard*. My sister guilted me into going again, though, and I'm glad she did, because I've now been hooked for years.

There's one more thing that I know helps, but that I have the hardest time with: cutting out my cell phone, computer, and iPad in the evenings. Scientifically, these devices inhibit our sleeping patterns due to the artificial blue light that the screens produce, which suppresses the secretion of melatonin. Your body naturally starts secreting melatonin before bedtime, so that by the time you lie in bed you're set to doze off into dreamland. When we stare at our phones all night, this never happens and, in essence, we are actively telling our bodies that it's not time to sleep yet.

Different things keep me from turning off my devices at a reasonable hour. The most important one is that my family and my friends are my lifeline, and none of them live close to me. We stay in touch via text, sometimes late into the night and, in the end, I would choose that over normal sleep patterns.

I'm also, as we've discussed, self-employed, which means there's no one else around to take calls/emails on my behalf. Finally, jotting down words in a notepad isn't going to cut it when it comes to being a writer. As I type this exact sentence, it's 9:33 p.m. on a

Sunday night, which means that even if I stopped right now I'd most likely still be screwed until sometime after midnight.

Over time I began to realize that my lack of sleep and my mounting stress levels were things that I needed to stop blaming on the chaos that we call life. Yes, stressful situations will arise and, yes, sometimes we'll be completely wired. It's inevitable that we'll miss a good night's sleep here and there because of the many things on our minds. It all goes back to the age-old reminder of controlling what we can, and letting go of what we can't. We need to recognize our triggers, our patterns and what holds us back because, many times, the only thing that stands in our way is ourselves and our habits.

Eventually, I'll learn to put my electronic devices away in the evenings, and I'm sure when that happens, I'll see some major improvement in my sleep patterns. Okay, maybe. That would be so much easier if I wasn't such a night owl, especially a night owl that feels more and more focused the later it gets.

What I learned...you know what, apparently nothing. It's 11:08 p.m. as I'm typing this, on an electronic device.

You know what, let's just move on.

FIFTEEN

Yes, And...

Improv is fascinating. It's a form of comedy that is challenging, hilarious and unlike any other form of performing. There is no way to prepare for any given scene, other than to rely on the principles of improvisation as you've learned them and to trust in your scene partner that he/she will do the same.

Improvisation is defined as something that is created without preparation. No preconceived notions about what should or may happen, just a completely-in-the-moment situation that plays out however it does.

When studying improv, there are a few rules. The most important thing that you're taught is to listen to your scene partner and respond *only* to what he or she has said, always taking what they say and applying the "yes, and" principle. This means that no matter what they've said, they're right, you go with it and enable the scene to further develop. For example, if they say you're in a coffee shop, you're in a coffee shop and ugh! Maybe your coffee just burned your tongue. If they say you're not the sharpest tool in the shed maybe you ask why there are tools in sheds because you're just kinda hungry.

The biggest challenge that I've had in improv is getting out of my own head. If the audience gives you a suggestion, it's so easy to start quickly scripting something in your mind of what you think might be funny. This, though, is a surefire way to absolutely derail any scene that you're working with, as there is no way for your partner to see that script and there's no time to fill him or her in. So, you and your partner are immediately not on the same page and pretty soon you're just firing off nonsense and hoping the other person will figure it out.

The above scenario had a very similar feeling to many heated conversations that I've been in. There have definitely been times in which I have a very clear point of view, and I have a list of bullet points in my mind about why my thoughts are the correct ones. Instead of listening and responding to what the other person is saying, therefore respecting their feelings and in turn, respecting myself by also doing what's best for me, I would half-listen and then do my best to convince them why maybe how they were feeling wasn't valid. Here's an example (fake, but realistic) transcript of how something like that may have looked.

Him: I don't like olives.

Me: (loves olives) you just haven't tried good olives. Try these, you'll love them.

Him: No, I really don't like olives. I've tried them many times.

Me: (loves olives. Doesn't understand how anyone can not like olives) ok for me. Just try this one and if you hate it I'll never ask you to try one again.

Him: (tries olive because he likes me. hates it. throws up. lunch is ruined.)

If you're close with someone, it should be expected that there is a certain level of trust that exists. If that's the case, then, you should be confident that you can take what they say at face value. I can look back on countless conversations with people that I trusted in which I heard what they said and then tried to convince them that

116

that's not really how they felt. I've been on the receiving end of that, as well. I don't think causing harm is the root of that situation, I think we all just have our times when we think we know best.

I'm not kidding you, improv has completely changed how I approach things in that area. It's shocking how efficiently a conversation can go if you're actually fully listening to the other person before you respond. Furthermore, I am so much more calm about things. I figured out why this was after watching an interview with Lisa Kudrow about her time at The Groundlings, where I've studied.

Kudrow began to talk about how great it was to have people who would be direct with you, a train of thought I was immediately on board with. In Los Angeles, people tell you that things were great when they weren't or that they really liked something when they didn't, probably for reasons including avoiding confrontation. That's great, but I can't work with that. If you don't like something, give it to me straight so that I can work on it and make it better.

She then went on to say something that resonated with me wholeheartedly:

"As I got into the mindset of what improvisation was, I understood - like, forget acting - that's what you need for life. You have to really listen. And really respond to what's been said. And the mindset is whatever is said, it's okay. Whatever is said, it's okay! It's fine. It's good. It's good!"

Wow, I thought. Maybe it could really be that easy. Just like in improv, I needed to go through life with the mindset that whatever happened, it was good. It was good because I could work with it and respond appropriately, *whatever* that meant. Good or bad, stressful or happy.

Here's how the above scenario may look in the improv mindset.

> *Him: I don't like olives.*
>
> *Me: (loves olives) Really?! Oh my gosh, I love olives. Have you ever tried good olives?*
>
> *Him: Yep, I've just tried them many times and I can't stand them.*
>
> *Me: Ahh! That's how I am with Brussel sprouts.*
>
> *Him: I love Brussel sprouts!*

During class at The Groundlings, we may get a suggestion for a location, a relationship, or a profession. And that's all we'll get. So, picture this: Two people stand on an empty stage, and are given a tiny piece of information. The audience (your classmates) applauds. Then, you've gotta make something happen. And the best things happen when you make a character choice and make direct eye contact with your scene partner, being able to figure out where they're at with nothing more than their body language, facial expressions and the look in their eyes.

The things that I try to do in every improv scene have become the things I try to do in every interpersonal situation off stage: trust, listen and live in the now. In improv, it's essential to trust your scene partner and to only focus on what they've *just* said, not what they're going to say later in the scene. Similarly, it makes it so much easier when you focus on what's happening around you *right this minute* and not try to plan for something that may or may not happen days or weeks down the road. Many different factors can change the outcome of every single situation you may be faced with. So, unless you're a psychic, it's literally impossible to predict. It's definitely easier said than done, and something I have to remind myself every day, but it sure does allow for a lot less stress.

Imagine every relationship in your life. The ones that stress you out, the ones that you don't fully understand, the ones that make you genuinely happy.

What I learned is the importance of going in to every single conversation with the intention of truly listening to everything that the other person is saying, both non-verbally and verbally, and only responding to that. And knowing that whatever comes out of their mouths, *it's okay. It's good!* You can now move forward.

SIXTEEN

Extroverted Introvert

I am directly in the middle of the introvert/extrovert spectrum, which I learned after taking the Myers-Briggs personality test. If you've never taken it, I highly recommend doing so. It's a psychology-based personality assessment that assigns you a four-letter personality type based on your answers to simple questions, and then breaks down your answers into one of 16 personality types. It's pretty spot on and really helps you understand yourself and those around you better. There are a few free websites you can use to judge your type, including HumanMetrics.com.

I've taken it probably 20 times, and have always gotten the same results, which puts me smack dab on the border of the I(ntrovert)NFJ and E(xtrovert) personalities. I've also made most of my friends and family take it because I was a psychology major and, well, these things interest me.

The best way I've come to describe how it feels to be on the border of being introverted and extroverted is that, while I do like socializing and being in a social environment, afterwards I need a solid amount of time to decompress and lay low. To rejuvenate, I suppose you could say.

This kind of thing can be very confusing for those around me. Sometimes I will be texting and socializing like it's my job (which sometimes it is), and sometimes I will be keeping to myself and writing, playing video games or watching whatever is on my DVR (probably *Vanderpump Rules*).

As I mentioned, I moved to Ann Arbor and completely kept to myself. I didn't really even think about going out and trying to make friends and, therefore, I didn't make friends - until someone else saw something in me that broke me out of my shell a little bit. The same thing happened at Google and then in the entertainment industry. On any given set, especially when I first started, I could usually be found alone in my green room between breaks instead of chatting with the crew. I would usually also eat lunch by myself and, if there was a shorter break between takes, I'd just kinda sit on my phone in the corner.

I *am* social. I like to chat and I genuinely like getting to know people. If I can help someone or support someone, it brings me joy in life. So it's kinda confusing, even for me, that I have such introverted tendencies. Especially for someone who feels alive when in front of a camera speaking to millions of viewers.

It's not because I didn't want to make friends, it's because there is this weird part of me that is painfully shy when I'm in a new situation. And I'm telling you all of this because I feel like there is so much pressure to be social, make friends, and put a happy image out there and I beat myself up for not feeling like I was living up to the social nature of our world.

I met one of my best friends in the world on the set of a horrible comedic short. I was keeping to myself as usual when Christina sat next to me and started chatting. I was very jaded at the time, and admittedly didn't think much of it because no one really seems to make friends on one-day shoots in Los Angeles. I don't know why. You're together for 14 hours and people are nice enough, but people are mostly there to further their career, do their job, and leave.

On a long break between scenes, we bonded over similar interests and how neither of us were from Los Angeles, but that we both loved what we were doing, despite the struggles that we faced in the industry. We hit it off almost immediately and vowed to hang out soon.

Over the next *two years*, which happened to be the stretch just before my 30th birthday when I was especially in my introverted hole, she never gave up on our friendship even though I had blown her off so many times. I'd take forever to respond to a text, be too wrapped up in relationship drama or be on the road when she wanted to have lunch but somehow, every few months, she'd send me a text just saying hi and saying she'd love to get together sometime.

Lucky for me, she's a complete extrovert. She gets her energy from being around other people, and I assume that was part of the reason that she continued to reach out. I'm infinitely thankful that she did, because she became my sanity.

Come to think of it, most lasting friendships of mine have happened slowly over time, and I usually don't make much of an effort at first. It's not at all because I don't have an interest in getting to know other people, I absolutely do - but as I've gotten older, I've gone more and more into my shell. This was especially interesting when I entered the baseball world. I, quite honestly, had no idea what I was getting into. I'll tell you how this all came about in the next chapter, but while we're on the topic of socialization, I think it's a good time to talk about life in the stands.

You may be familiar with the term "WAGS." It stands for "wives and girlfriends" and it's supposedly limited to the sports industry. I'm not particularly fond of this term, partially because the lifestyle has been completely glamorized thanks to reality shows and the perceived incredible lifestyles of women who are dating or are married to a man who plays sports. Let me be clear: I am not saying this lifestyle sucks. I'm simply saying it's not always what it's portrayed to be.

First of all, it's really not as glamorous as you may think. These guys work their asses off to get to the big leagues, and, if they do make it, it's because they've persevered through the ups and downs of professional sports. They've earned their spot through hard work, dedication, and an unwavering competitive spirit.

Second, they simply don't have the time to be dealing with the logistics of the unpredictability of the business, such as finding a new place to live or figuring out the best schools for the kids. When it comes to baseball, they play 162 games a year, minimum. They have 12 total off days from April to early October, and the hope is that the season goes longer than that, into the playoffs. They're also at the field for probably 10 hours a day.

And so, the women are the ones planning for each move, making sure the kids have their routines and doing their best to make their man feel comfortable and focused during the eight, nine, ten month baseball season.

It's easy to think, "Isn't that the other partner's job, when the other one is working and providing all of the income?" Some may agree. But it's so much more complicated than that.

Stepping in to the group of girls, first in Seattle and then in Chicago, it was a shock. It was a shock because I, having socially awkward tendencies and being completely overwhelmed with Mike's sudden trade from the Mariners to the Cubs, was now sitting with women for three to four hours each day. I tried my best to not be weird, but I did just kinda chill and watch the games for the first few months.

It's nothing like you see on TV. Each baseball family has different things to deal with and each woman has their battles, successes and stresses. Many are young mothers, raising kids on the go. Some are the wives of superstars and, whether they like it or not, their lives are constantly on display and susceptible to criticism and hate on social media like you wouldn't believe (and they did not, in fact, ask for the scrutiny that they receive). Other women may have done the heavy lifting of moving four or more times in one year. And most have made immense sacrifices when it comes to their own career and/or life plans in order to be with the man they love.

Baseball, like other lucrative and highly competitive careers, has a way of testing you and making sure you submit to it before you're able to figure out how to adapt. And the only way I found that

I was able to adapt was to find comfort in what the other girls around me had gone through, knowing that I wasn't alone.

I'm still uncomfortable in new social situations sometimes. And that's okay. *What I learned* is that no one's life is as perfect as it may look from the outside, and everyone has things that they're dealing with, in baseball or outside of it. And speaking of baseball, let's get into how it all began.

SEVENTEEN

Mike

When it comes to romance, I want to put it out there that casual dating has never been for me. I don't know why. I admire people who put themselves out there, but the thought of even going to dinner or grabbing a cup of coffee with someone made me uncomfortable. I just didn't see the point - I wasn't actively looking for someone to be with and I could buy my own coffee. Spoken like an emotionally closed off champion, am I right?

I'd dated people along the way, and none of them were particularly wonderful relationships. My last relationship was the worst one, and left me with no interest whatsoever in dating. There I was, fully prepared to be a single, career woman for however long that may have been.

Lucky me, though, being 30 and single meant that everyone and their mother felt the need to ask me what I was "trying" at the moment, if I had plans to get married in the future and then telling me not to worry, because I will *definitely* find someone great at some point.

Just as I tried to figure out what "trying" means, the inevitable questions soon followed. Am I on dating sites? How do I usually meet men? Have I tried Match.com? No, woman at a social function, that I barely know, that I think may be friends with my mom...I have not tried Match nor do I have any desire to and Tinder is something straight out of my nightmares.

Most of my adult life, I've worked tirelessly to build my career. It became clear that my ideal relationship would include someone who is willing to share my vision of why I've worked so hard to get where I am, and who would never want me to give that up - all while trusting that they would be loved and taken care of in the way that they deserve to be.

I knew Mike was "my person" from the beginning. I didn't know that I knew, but I knew. It was this weird, quizzical feeling that there was something about this guy who was acting too cool for school, even though he looked at me the same way I looked at him when we asked each other about our lives. The look I'm describing is a mix of skepticism (are you as good as I think you might be?), confusion (why are you different than other people I've met?) and intrigue (I want to know more about you.).

I met this freakin' guy on Twitter in 2015. ON TWITTER. How embarrassing. He doesn't think it's embarrassing, because that's "just how things happen nowadays," but the whole thing just makes no sense.

It took me a while to figure out how the connection was even made. We didn't follow each other, nor did I follow any athletes or celebrities. Turns out I liked a tweet that he was mentioned in, and because I had a certain amount of followers he got the "Stephanie Duchaine liked a tweet you were mentioned in!" notification. Lucky for me, those were the days when I had more followers than he did and he still had his notifications turned on.

After apparently asking his teammates in Seattle if any of them "knew me" (read: had slept with me) he asked them how to get my attention. One of his teammates at the time suggested that he like one of my tweets. And thus began our courtship.

We started chatting, and he eventually told me I should come meet him for a drink. At the time, I lived in Los Angeles but was up visiting my parents in Seattle and he played for the Seattle Mariners.

Regardless of the perfect timing, I laughed to myself and wrote him back that I was watching a movie and going to bed. "What movie?" he asked. *Draft Day*, I responded.

He asked if I wanted him to leave me a ticket for the game the next day and I thought - who the heck is this guy, and how many tickets has he left for random chicks he met on Twitter? The logical part of my brain said to stay home, but I told him that I would go. I'd been single for well over a year, without so much as a single date - so I figured worst-case scenario I'd go watch a baseball game and have a drink with someone who might at least have some interesting stories to tell.

He acted so casual about the whole thing. We sat in the bar at Morton's, where we ended up grilling each other about the status of our lives. I told him about my career while he told me about some of the struggles he'd faced in the minors, and what it was like to go back and forth. I was, admittedly, fascinated. I knew nothing about him or the true struggles of a professional athlete.

Dinner turned to the bar, the bar turned into 4 a.m. drunk conversations, which turned into breakfast the next day. I remember leaving, turning around and waving to him thinking, "I'll never see that guy again." I went home and told my mom that he was funny and we had a great time, but that I'd never date him.

I mean, come on. He was younger than me. We lived in different cities, and, even though I somehow had the ability to see right through his cool guy exterior, I genuinely figured that life circumstances alone were enough to make it not worth pursuing.

Naturally, most of my friends and family felt the same way. He was almost (by 5 days, so yes, almost) five years younger than me and was at the pivotal point in his career where he was going to make it to the majors or be in a real tough situation.

Two days later, I got a text. We hung out again, and again. I conveniently booked trips to Seattle so that I could see him while I "just happened to be there for work or to see my family."

The next six months were rough, I'm not gonna lie to you. I was traveling an insane amount for work, while watching his outings on MLB.tv from Florida, California and even Paris. There was one game that started at 4 a.m. Parisian time. I went to the store down the street and got some cheese and a baguette, preparing myself to stay awake and watch his outing.

He got absolutely lit up. He gave up something like seven runs in a few innings and by 4:30 a.m., he'd been pulled and it was time for bed. I texted him to let him know that I was thinking about him and that if it was easy, everyone would do it. He responded that everyone has bad days and that he just had to look to the future.

Little did I know that there was pitch calling, plan changing and internal chaos going on that resulted in some struggles, followed by a demotion to AAA Tacoma in August. He wasn't called back up in September, either - regardless of the fact that he'd thrown two back-to-back complete game shutouts earlier in the season. As a rookie! Dude made history, then finished the season in AAA.

In the 2015 offseason, he was told that he most likely didn't have a place on the team, and was offered a chance to play in Japan. The money was good, and it was only for a season. We hadn't been together long enough for me to give my input, but when he asked my opinion I told him that if I needed to get on a plane to Japan, I would. But that I also believed in him enough that whatever he wanted to do, I knew he'd succeed.

He said no to the first offer, and was then offered double the amount. Compared to a minor league salary, this was life-changing money - that he turned down because he believed he had what it took to succeed in Major League Baseball. The M's told him that there were no guarantees, but that he could compete for a roster spot in spring.

He proved himself in spring training, and was given his first opening day roster spot as a member of the bullpen. For the Mariners in 2016, he ended up being a swingman and posted a 2.34 ERA over 61.2 innings pitched. I thought we had it made - my family was in Seattle, he was living the dream, and so was I.

In a shocking twist of events, a family friend was getting married on a Saturday night and I was actually able to bring him as a date after a day game! This never happens during baseball season.

Baseball wives and girlfriends will tell you that they go solo to most baseball season weddings, if they're able to go at all.

He was starting the next day and broke his routine, for me. And let me be clear, he has a routine. He eats a good meal, he doesn't drink, and he plays Xbox for hours because, he says, Xbox is "a way to stay competitive without the risk of injury." See - he *needs* to play for hours a day. It's good for the team.

I picked him up at Safeco Field and we drove to the wedding, which happened to be just down the street. It was mid-July and I was thrilled that my entire family was together. Mike didn't have so much as one beer, and we were headed home by 8:30 p.m.

He started the next day. The defense gave up four errors - which absolutely should have been five considering the ball hit the outfielder's glove and dropped to the ground (yes, I'm still bitter. At the situation, not the players. Baseball is hard!). I later heard whispers of how he was spotted at a wedding the night before, which "probably wasn't smart before a start." This was my first lesson in everything these guys do being scrutinized, even when they're trying to do things for their families/significant others.

All things considered, he had been a huge asset to the team. From being told he had no spot to stepping into whatever they needed him to do, he did what he had to without bitching, whining or complaining. They said jump, he said how high - but regardless of how far he'd come in the last year, his greatest adventure was yet to come.

I was at Bible study in a conference room upstairs at Safeco, which the team coordinated for the wives and girlfriends. He wasn't pitching, but my entire family was in the stands watching the game. Nothing but a calm, normal day at the field.

The group was small that day - four, maybe five people. We finished our session and I opened my eyes with a smile.

Out of nowhere, I hear: "Stephanie. Oh my gosh. Steph. Oh my…"

"What? What's going on?" I said, startled by the sudden change in tone.

One of the girls slid her phone across the table as mine, screen side down, was on Do Not Disturb lying on the table.

The alert read: "LHP Mike Montgomery traded to the Chicago Cubs." I flipped my phone over to a million alerts, text messages and missed calls. I went into shock and sat there frozen, as I looked up to the TV in the corner that was playing the game on mute. A mere 10 seconds later, a clubhouse assistant was seen tapping Mike's shoulder in the dugout in the 6th inning, motioning to the clubhouse as the announcers, which I read in closed caption, announced that he was being told he was traded.

I texted him and told him that I was heading down to the tunnel and that I would be there whenever he was ready to come out. He responded, "You heard?"

Holy shit. I realized that he was one of the last people to know. "Yes, I heard." I replied. "What do you think?" he asked. "I think you're going to win a World Series earlier than anticipated." (This is a true statement. I am basically psychic and called it on July 20th, 2016.)

The next 24 hours were a whirlwind. He left the next morning to meet the team in Milwaukee and my parents and I packed up his entire apartment into his truck, which we then took to Safeco to be shipped to Chicago. We then had just enough time to get an early dinner before they dropped me at SeaTac to fly back to L.A. in time for a shoot the next day.

I, quite frankly, became his assistant in that time. There was a lot of ugly crying going on. You're talking about an independent woman who had been previously unwilling to rely on a man in any way, who was also suddenly forced to make a big decision. Make sacrifices and commit to this person, or don't. Baseball really doesn't allow for it to happen any other way.

I didn't know how the hell it could possibly work, but I started with packing up his apartment. We didn't live together at the time, but, when you're traded, you're out. He packed a bag, flew out to meet the Cubs in Milwaukee and I met him in Chicago for his Cubs debut the week after.

It became pretty clear that if I wanted this to work, at such a vital time in his career, I was going to have to be the one to make some career sacrifices. This was a personal choice, that I sometimes struggle with but I never regret. I was given the opportunity to move to New York and host a show four days a week, but I declined. After everything I'd been through in my career, *I declined.* And oh my, did I get judged for it. How could I, an independent woman who had worked so hard to get where I was, give it up (on any level) for a man? That's just *sad.*

You know what? I *was* a little sad to be faced with these decisions. But every decision that I've made, I stand behind. I wasn't willing to be away from the first guy I've ever seen a real future with for weeks at a time, and so, I decided to say goodbye to life as I knew it. The life of a sole career woman, with no focus on kids, pets or anyone else. A woman who was only interested in growing her career, at the expense of the other amazing things that life has to offer.

Sometimes we have to make hard decisions and, contrary to popular belief, this does not make us sell-outs. I didn't sacrifice my career, though it may have felt like it for a hot second. I simply took a little hiatus, and then got creative. It's never too late to reinvent yourself based on your changing circumstances - and your circumstances will, most likely, forever be changing.

Getting creative and being open to an eventual change led me to an ongoing commercial series, live TV spots on a major Chicago network and...wait for it...finally publishing a book. Not to mention getting married and being blessed with two amazing children.

What I learned is that at some point in your life, you will have enough previous experience to be able to go with the flow. Your life as you know it may implode, but you'll know yourself well enough to know what you need to do to adapt and it's never, ever too late to try something new. It might be a job change, a new relationship or having a kid - but when the time is right you'll know deep down what you gotta do, and you'll do it.

EIGHTEEN

108 Years

Picture this. You're the new guy, and you don't know anyone on your new team. You don't know the city, you've never pitched in the ballpark. You were told you'd probably be spending that year in Japan and now here you were, contending for a World Series.

Given that Mike had only been in the American League, he had never experienced the rivalry that is Cubs/Brewers, but he learned very quickly what it was all about when he gave up a bomb to the first batter he faced for his new team, at Miller Park. He also learned just how passionate Chicago fans are, and how quickly they'll tell you their thoughts on Twitter. This was when he had to turn notifications off to avoid his home screen being overwhelmed with messages.

He'd been traded before while in the minors, but this was different. A different stage with different expectations. Being programmed to be a robot with laser focus, it was hard to give himself any grace to transition and, being that it was end of July, there was very little leeway from the fans who had waited a literal lifetime for a World Series.

After a few weeks, he began to find his groove and, before we knew it, it was mid-September and the Cubs clinched the division. A few more weeks went by and we found ourselves in the playoffs. It was an "even year" so the Giants were confident that they'd shut the Cubs down, given that they'd already won the Series in 2010, 2012 and 2014.

I was never a Giants fan, but having lived in San Francisco I was looking forward to getting back to AT&T park. I started to look for flights to the away games just as Mike got home from the field and let me know that the organization was flying the wives, girlfriends and children to all of the away games.

"*What?*" I asked. "Who does that?"

The Cubs do that.

Chicago is something special, man. Let me tell you. You feel the vibe as soon as you walk through the gates at Wrigley. Walking into the stands from the concourse it was almost immediately solidified as my favorite park in baseball. Couple that with the fact that the organization is top notch, and I began to understand what John Kinsella felt in *Field of Dreams* when he asked if he was in heaven.

From the NLDS on, they flew the wives, girlfriends and children on a chartered plane to all away games so that the dudes could have their squad with them. This is just one example of their generosity - they cater meals for the families before every game. They plan monthly wives/girlfriends outings. And, among numerous other things, they never once made me, a girlfriend, feel less than a wife. Which, even if you've been together for years, isn't always the norm in baseball. Some organizations don't even allow fiancées the same privileges as wives.

The Cubs won the first two games of the NLDS, and off we went to San Francisco. It's a three out of five series, so we just needed one more win to solidify our spot in the NLCS.

Game three was the worst. Mike came in for the 9th inning when the game was tied, and pitched 4+ scoreless innings before giving up a run in the 13th inning. He was destroyed over it. He couldn't help but feel like he'd let the team down when, in reality, he sustained the team for as long as he possibly could. After being so close to clinching the series, the fire was relit the next day.

I didn't know anything that was happening until about the eighth inning of game four. Fun fact: I can't eat spinach. Unbeknownst to me, I'd chosen a great time to ingest it when I unknowingly ate a nice Caesar wrap in a spinach tortilla before the game. So, I spent a solid two hours of the game in the hospital that I didn't know existed at AT&T Park, where I took some extra strength Benadryl and tried to throw up. What'd I tell you? Baseball isn't always glamorous.

In the bottom of the eighth inning, Mike's parents texted me that they were leaving. They said the mojo wasn't there and, being superstitious, they wanted to leave and switch things up. I said okay, and that I was going down to the family waiting area to sit by myself.

There was no TV down there, and I was by myself with the exception of the Almora's new baby and his grandparents. In my Benadryl daze, I checked my phone and saw that it was 5-2 after the bottom of the eighth. It seemed like it was about to be a long ride home to Chicago, where we'd have to win this thing in five.

Not much time had passed when someone poked his head into the family room doorway and said "Just so you know, they just tied it up. You might not want to miss this."

My spinach allergy doesn't do nice things to my body. It passes in a few hours, but in the meantime it feels like I'm rotating between a freezer and pure hell, while the inside of my body is being wrung like a wet rag. Pleasant, I know. I usually end up crying from the pain, and the only thing that usually helps is an antihistamine and an anti-nausea pill, both of which usually put me to sleep.

Especially after the night before, when Mike worked his ass off trying to get his team to the next level, I knew this wasn't something I should miss. I had to see how this game was going to end. I had red eyes, messy hospital bed hair and didn't know what day it was, but I made my way to the seats in right field just in time to see Javy Baez get the eventual game winning RBI before Aroldis Chapman struck out the side to win it in the bottom of the ninth.

After the initial celebrations, Mike came out of the clubhouse to kiss me and give me a beer. He had no idea that his parents had left or that I'd missed half the game. It probably wasn't the smartest idea, but the carbonation (and probably the alcohol) actually helped, and after my Benadryl/Budweiser cocktail, we eventually flew back to Chicago.

We played the Dodgers in the NLCS. The Dodgers won two of the first three games, but the Cubs went on to win the series in six. The away games were the only games in the playoffs that I couldn't make, as I was shooting a series on the East Coast. The team looked incredible, and I was screaming in my hotel room as I watched Mike get a single and the win during game four. It was a great week.

Don't get me wrong, I've been in some high pressure situations in my life. I've alpha tested the Android software. I've given up a stable job to be self-employed, and I've been on live television in front of millions of people. My first hosting job was in the first position on the red carpet (meaning the celebrities are contractually obligated to talk to you first), interviewing Victoria Beckham and Eva Longoria. I legitimately thought I was going to pass out or pee my pants.

I don't know, though, if I've ever been as stressed out as I was before game one of the World Series in Cleveland, Ohio.

Mike is pretty stoic. He always has been. Despite his best efforts I can usually tell if there's something bothering him, and that morning there were no signs of anything. He was a little cocky (I call this being "big man,") but he wasn't carrying the weight of the city of Chicago, nor was he focused on everything that could go wrong. He was just trying to go out and execute pitches.

Me, on the other hand - I was a damn mess. I remember walking down to the lobby to meet his parents later in the afternoon, and my head was spinning so much I could barely see straight. I was looking at this series emotionally and I didn't know how to handle it. A few months before, we were in Seattle. Nine months before, he was told he would be better off in Japan. Now here we were, a part of the biggest World Series in the history of baseball.

After three games, the series was 2-1 in favor of the Indians, and I'll never forget game four. Mike, who prides himself in fielding comebackers, was on the mound when a ball was hit back to him. As he went to catch it, the force of the ball took his glove off and by the time he recovered and went to throw to first, the runner had made it safely to first base.

The Cubs went on to lose that game and fell to 3-1 in the series. Usually, no matter what had happened in the game, Mike gets in the car and maintains a positive attitude. He'll admit that he felt a little off or that he didn't have one of his pitches that night, but he'll say "I feel good, it was just one of those nights you have to learn from and move on from!"

When he got in the car the night of game four, though, he was quiet. He then told me that he had never believed in curses, but that when the ball hit his glove and flew off, which had never happened in the history of his career, he was beginning to believe.

I told him to relax. We both knew that they were about to fight an uphill battle, but if there was ever a team that was set up for an unbelievable comeback, it was the 2016 Chicago Cubs.

That night, he stayed up in a frustrated state playing NHL 2017. In his last game, around 4 a.m., he was down 3-1 in the 3rd period with three minutes left. He was swearing and starting to lose his shit when (and I can't make this shit up), he scored three goals to win the game 4-3. I told him if that wasn't a sign then I didn't know what was, and I went to bed.

Well, they won game five. And if you've never been to Wrigley, I can't even begin to tell you what it felt like to be there for that. Wrigley is magical. I've sat through games where the weather is absolutely miserable (40 degrees with sideways, windy rain) and I still didn't hate it. Cut to October baseball in gorgeous, unseasonable weather, and I dare you to find anything better.

Here we go, back to Cleveland, where we won game six. Pretty soon we're right back in it, and we were doing everything we could to stay in the "another day, another game" mindset. He was playing his video games on his portable player and we ordered room service - yep, nothing to see here.

And then the day has come. It's game seven. I'm completely numb by this point. I literally can't feel my face, and it's not because I'm drunk, it's because I have no idea what's going on other than the fact that I had fried chicken at 2 a.m. the night before and it was delicious.

I want you to know that I'm drinking Scotch as I relive this moment. I don't even drink Scotch, but it's 12:48 a.m. on a Friday and I am riled up just thinking about November 2nd, 2016.

I said goodbye to Mike that morning in our usual fashion of a kiss and "bye babe, have a good day." I tried to keep it casual and said "good luck tonight" like it was just a standard Tuesday.

Whether or not you're even a sports fan, that game was absolutely insane. Insane, I tell you. After starting with a Dexter Fowler leadoff home run, the Cubs were up 5-1 in the 5th inning. It started to look like we had this in the bag.

I should have known better. I never, ever think games are in the bag until they're over. I don't care if it's the 7th inning and we're up by 10, I keep my mouth shut.

When the Indians' Rajai Davis hit the homer in the eighth to tie the score at 6, I went more numb than I already had been. I forgot what day it was, and where I was. My shoulders slouched and I slowly sat in my seat trying to process what just happened. It's not that I felt like the Cubs were going to lose. It's that I didn't understand how the hell the rollercoaster just. kept. going. Win in a blowout? LOL! Throw the life plan in the trash can, people!

All right, so the game is tied. It's the most high stress game I've ever been to, and absolutely the most high stress game I've ever been this invested in. Aroldis Chapman had come back out for the ninth, and pitched a scoreless inning. Tensions were so high, I don't know how anyone was maintaining their sanity in that moment. And then, as if on cue, it started to rain.

The rest of the game was a blur. After the rain delay, the Cubs scored two runs to take the lead. We were three outs away. As we headed to the bottom of the 10th, I was counting the number of relievers left in the pen. We've only got a few, and Mike is one of them. I'm not even thinking of how this is going to go down because if you've watched any of Joe Maddon's games, there's no use predicting.

The Indians weren't going to go down without a fight, and scored a run to make it 8-7. And then with two outs and a runner on first, here comes Maddon.

Oh no, I wonder. *What's he going to do?*

In no time at all, there he is. I see Mike's signature, left leg hop on his first step out of the bullpen and then here he comes, making that slow jog out to the mound.

Let me be clear - my faith in him never wavered. I knew he was tired, but I also knew what he was capable of and what a competitor he was. But shit man, it's baseball. Anything can happen. A base hit. An error. A bad call.

Mike's parents are behind me, and none of us are speaking to each other. They've spent their lives following his career, including eight years in the minors, his MLB debut, AAA demotion and trade to Chicago. I've been in the picture for far less time, but my investment went from 0-60 in a way that I never could have expected.

He toes the mound and sets up for pitch number one. Curveball. Michael Martinez took the pitch, for strike one.

What the hell, man. Someone slap me, I can't feel my face again.

In a whirlwind of a next pitch, he elicited a ground ball to Kris Bryant, who slipped on the wet grass just enough to make every Cubs fan around the world gasp for breath. A split second later, the ball was in Rizzo's glove and that was it. The next thing I remember was seeing Mike's long arms in the middle of the dog pile. Is it still a dog pile if no one is on the ground? I say no, but Mike says yes. So I'll go with it.

Mike's baseball career is an amazing example of what happens when you go with the flow and have faith in yourself. After being a first-round pick, he spent eight years in the minors. After making his debut and throwing back-to-back complete game shutouts, was later told he wouldn't make the team and he should take a spot on the team in Japan. When he said no, he was told that he may not make the roster and could be put on waivers.

What I learned is that he is a perfect example of throwing a life plan in the trash can. He was *so close* so many times, only to face a setback. Part of what drew me to him, though, was his unwavering determination - which over the course of a decade led him from the minors, to a potential release, to throwing the last pitch in one of the most incredible World Series of all time.

NINETEEN

A Medium-Sized Dog

After the insanity that was 2016, the following year would be considered by some to be unremarkable. The Cubs lost in the NLCS to the Dodgers, after winning the NLDS in five games in Washington, DC. From my perspective, the year was filled with accomplishments.

After the shortest offseason in baseball, the Cubs made it further than 26 other teams. Each guy on that team had powered through injuries and fatigue and they fought like hell to beat the best teams in the country. In Mike's case, he had pitched 30 more innings in the 2017 regular season than he had in the previous year. He hit his first career home run in June and he was an extremely versatile swingman for the team. But by October, he was exhausted.

After the Cubs lost game five, which was at Wrigley, we went back to the apartment and did nothing for a solid week. Mike played video games and I watched TV. We disconnected from the world and felt like we had the ability to decompress for the first time in two years. We started prepping to move to Arizona for the offseason…but not before we added a new member to the family.

Mike is a "dog person." He's wanted a dog for as long as I've known him, but situationally it just wasn't feasible. I had an apartment in Los Angeles and I was traveling back and forth every few weeks, on top of trips to New York, Louisville and wherever else I was working. He, of course, was on the road for weeks at a time and at the field for hours each day.

Earlier in the 2017 season, I had to put Fifi down. It was terrible. As the months went by, we started to consider getting a pet as I felt the void of my furry friend, and after two years we'd also started to perfect our baseball/entertainment balancing act. Most of my clients were then aware of the fact that Mike played baseball and they've been incredibly great at working around my insane schedules. One client even saw me cry when I was watching the game in Atlanta on my iPad during a shooting break when Mike hit his first career homer.

Mike actually surprised me with how much research he wanted to do. He was adamant that we needed to research breeds, behaviors, even gender characteristics of dogs before we looked into getting one. His reasoning was that with both of our schedules, the fact that we move at least twice a year and that as of now the living space in Chicago was an apartment, it wouldn't be fair to us or to the dog if we didn't do our due diligence.

After charts, lists and a full-on breed bracket, we started to feel like maybe the miniature Australian Shepherd would be the right breed for us. They're adaptable, 35-40 pounds and were initially bred to be companions for cross country truckers.

Our research told us that in the United States, they dock (cut off) the tails at birth. Aussies are herders by nature, and docking the tail was initially to keep things from getting stuck in their tails when running around herding animals.

For a household pet, this is obviously not necessary, and I began Googling mini Aussies with tails. My research led me to a woman in Indiana named Angie who worked exclusively with mini Aussies and had a litter that had just been born in the UK, where it's illegal to dock tails.

Angie and her husband Bill were incredible to us. They invited us down to Indiana to meet mini Aussies from previous litters, many of whom lived nearby. We got to meet 10 different dogs, all of whom were friendly, loving and extremely smart. We told them all about our lifestyles and how we wanted to make sure we did our best to get a dog that would thrive in such an environment.

She said that she'd be going to England to do personality and temperament tests on the puppies at eight weeks old in order to best assign them homes. They don't allow someone to pick a dog based on color or aesthetic alone, as many Aussies can end up in the shelter if the owner isn't willing or able to keep up with the energy level, personality or responsibility of training.

After she went, she offered us a little fluff ball blue merle male, with speckled eyes and black markings on his gray and copper fur. We knew he was ours, and we said yes to getting him on November 3rd.

We named him Oliver Montgomery, and we call him Ollie for short. Ollie had an insane 24 hours. He was flown over from the UK, and we were then supposed to fly to Arizona with him a few hours later. He freaked out in the crate and, after stopping at a pet store before heading back to our terminal, we ended up missing what was the last flight out.

Poor little Ollie had no idea who we were, had just flown across the world and was separated from his siblings. He cried and cried, wanting nothing to do with our little carrier. He certainly had no interest in the hotel room that we ended up having to get at the airport after we rescheduled our 9 p.m. flight for a 5 a.m. one. None of us got any sleep that night, nor did we for the week after as we settled into our offseason routine.

We'd decided to spend the offseason in Arizona, both to have a yard for the pup and to not have to move in between three different cities that year. I got rid of my apartment and we have the best dog ever.

In the introduction of this book, I'd detailed the plan I'd made for myself when I was 15. The house, the acting career, the family life and even the medium-sized dog. While it looked nothing at all like that for so long and it certainly didn't happen by my mid-20s, almost 20 years later amid the twists and turns my vision doesn't seem that far off.

There were years of growing up in college, and years at Google. There were the ups and downs of the entertainment industry, risking my sanity and my welfare around every corner. And there were the ongoing thoughts that maybe there wasn't the perfect person out there for everyone.

Thirty three years later, I'm about to make the drive with Ollie to Chicago for the start of another baseball season. Two weeks after that, I'm flying to Louisville to continue shooting a commercial series. I certainly don't have all of the answers, but here's what I do know.

My dream of making it in the entertainment business, on any level, started as a far-fetched idea and seemed to slip further and further away from me with every passing month. I soon found myself years removed, having made no progress when it came to advancing in a lucrative, cutthroat industry.

It took Mike eight years in the minors to make it to his big league debut, where he found some great success, only to get sent back down to AAA.

And for 107 years, the Chicago Cubs did not win a World Series.

In every case, it would have been extremely easy to lose faith and let the dream fade away. It would have been so much easier to stay at Google, where I had a great setup - but it would have been at the expense of my lifelong dream.

For Mike, it would have been real easy to get pissed off and give up the game of baseball, losing the drive and determination when his time just didn't seem to come - but that would have been at the expense of being a part of World Series history.

And for Cubs fans everywhere, it would have been even easier to jump ship when the Cubs hadn't won a World Series in, well…ever.

By now, we all know - the best was yet to come.

What I learned was that if your heart says that you want something, it may take decades. It will most likely never, ever look the way you want it to or think that it will, and the path will be filled with rocks, peaks and valleys. But with patience, drive and determination, you may just end up having everything you ever wanted.

www.ingramcontent.com/pod-product-compliance
Lightning Source LLC
LaVergne TN
LVHW051102080426
835508LV00019B/2027